Unmentionables

Unmentionables

✦

A Woman's Journey, Body to Soul

Katherine T. Durack, Ph.D.

iUniverse, Inc.

New York Bloomington Shanghai

Unmentionables
A Woman's Journey, Body to Soul

iUniverse books may be ordered through booksellers or by contacting:

iUniverse
1663 Liberty Drive
Bloomington, IN 47403
www.iuniverse.com
1-800-Authors (1-800-288-4677)

ISBN: 978-0-595-48416-4 (pbk)
ISBN: 978-0-595-49645-7 (cloth)
ISBN: 978-0-595-60507-1 (ebk)

Printed in the United States of America

For the Saturday Morning Breakfast Group,
from whom I learned how powerful women speak.

Contents

PREFACE

While the lessons life teaches are not of our choosing, they are nevertheless indelibly inscribed in our flesh. Keeping silent about some wounds exacts a high price: when we don't speak, we lose the ability to do so.

I began the essays in this volume to recover my voice after losing it, both literally and figuratively. I had spent years trying to conform myself to the expectations of others: to teach how others thought I should teach, to write what others thought I should write, to be who others thought I should be. The result was predictable. I developed a stubborn case of laryngitis that threatened my ability teach my classes, to talk with my students during office hours, to talk with my husband and my friends after work.

Worse, for the first time in my life, I developed writer's block. This was devastating and potentially career-ending, as failing to publish either the right kind of book or the prescribed number of approved types of articles in the accepted academic journals would mean the end of my academic career. While I was accustomed to feeling somewhat awkward when speaking, I had always felt at home on the page, yet I couldn't bear to write another word of another essay that only a handful of people would ever read.

This is not the book the faculty hiring committee thought I would write during my years as a junior faculty member. Yet had I not given voice to these old wounds, had I not wondered aloud and on paper if I could still laugh at life and find humor in what troubled me, I can assure you the journey told here would certainly have had a different end. The moments I allowed myself each day to write, *first*, about what I felt most deeply gave me the ability to meet my commitments and to heal my voice.

What follows in these pages is part memoir and part commentary about female bodies and aging and voice. The events I describe actually happened, and in setting them down here I've tried to stick closely to the facts. I have changed the names of many people I mention and obscured some details whenever doing so does not compromise an underlying truth. For instance, because what has happened at one university is likely to have happened elsewhere, I make no distinction among the various campuses where different events occurred. Dialogue is emotionally accurate but may not be what others recall, given the inevitable colorings of intent, perception, and time. Throughout, the essays address what is unmentionable in our lives, the many subjects and situations about which women are expected to be silent.

1

MOUTH

I was from birth, like my siblings, gifted with a precocious volubility. I read voraciously—at college level by sixth grade. I told stories; I wrote poetry; I sang the songs my mother sang to me. So prolific were my outbursts that my father remarked I had "oral diarrhea"; more than once he told my mother to "shut that kid up." In response, I adopted mute forms of expression: I took up ballet and poured out my heart in class, in rehearsal, and on stage. I learned to be quiet in the company of others, cautious about speaking for the ire my words might provoke. I learned silence was essential to survival.

I remember the outcome rather than the substance of the argument: though I had retreated to my room when my father showed his furor, I paused halfway down the hall then returned to the fray. I pronounced respectfully but firmly, "I haven't said what I want to say," and I stated my position on the disagreement. Though I could see he ached to restrain himself, my impertinence provoked him and he struck me in the face for the first and only time. His hand, shaking with rage, barely grazed my cheek and mouth in the faintest shadow of violence that he himself had once received. But it was the fact of the blow more than its force that hurt. Tears traced my cheeks but I kept speaking; I left the room when I was done and moved out of the house the next day. We spoke again only months later when I told him of my successful audition for a Follies-style extravaganza at the MGM Grand Hotel in Las Vegas. With this job, I established my financial independence from my father, and as a result, I would not be coming along when the family left the country for his sabbatical the next fall.

The Vegas job was a good gig for a nineteen-year-old. It was about as stable a show business job as you could get: a year's contract with benefits, two free meals a day in the employee cafeteria, and a decent salary—after a couple of months of rehearsal pay ($150 per week), I would eventually earn almost $1,600 per month, what seemed to me then an extraordinary sum. I figured this would be a good way to find out if I really had the courage for a career on the stage, so I packed the pickup and left the Land of Enchantment for Sin City, the city of neon lights.

"Excuse me, sir," I asked timidly, "Could you please tell me specifically what it is I need to work on?" I was completely puzzled when the producer singled me out for criticism in the small group meetings he held with us that day. I'd just been promoted, from swing to singer, my second promotion since rehearsals had begun. I had earned the first promotion, from chorus dancer to swing, because of my ability to learn and execute choreography quickly; a swing dancer learns six roles and performs each on successive evenings when the regular dancers have a night off. The second promotion was largely a matter of luck: I got this role because I also had a pleasant singing voice—a delicate lyric soprano—and after over a month of rehearsals, one of the singers had quit. Eager to do well, I'd learned new choreography for the entire show in only a week. Though my body left the theatre at the end of rehearsals each day, my mind never did—I even dreamt the show when I slept. As far as I knew, I was making good progress learning the entire role, including the vocals.

Since the producer had kindly invited questions after our small group meeting, I was little prepared for the verbal onslaught my earnest request unleashed. Evil flooded the dimly lit theatre: It was as if my words had rent asunder the jaws of hell and out roared the venom and vituperation of all ages. His face clotted purple with fury: Every move I made was flawed;

I offended by my very being. I was deafened by the brutal blast and felt his words slash and scorch my tender flesh. I was profoundly silenced.

When I regained my senses, I boiled with rage that this producer had so foully condemned my honest efforts to excel. I vowed to show him wrong through the unassailable perfection of every step I took or note I sang on stage. I said not a word, but my body spoke my anger, and with each meticulous movement I dared him to find an error in my work. Yet even my silence was too bold: after one rehearsal, a seasoned dancer took me aside and cautioned me to change the attitude my body conveyed. I acquiesced—and within a few days lost my voice completely to laryngitis, thereby motivating further abuse when I was unable to answer a question from the producer about a traffic problem on stage. I stood at the apron of the stage and strained to issue any small sound that would satisfy the man; when after repeated badgering to answer a friend bravely volunteered that I had laryngitis and could not speak, he fired back that I could not sing either.

My own humiliation after seeking constructive criticism was nothing compared to events I later witnessed. I can scarcely imagine the kinds of threats—or the thugs who might have acted upon them—that could have reduced one of the principal dancers to offering a public apology in front of the entire cast and crew, over a hundred people. And the outrage that inspired such wrath? The principal dancer had committed the heinous crime of intervening when the producer savaged another cast member, and worse, revealed that several dancers gathered together to hold class before rehearsals. As the producer demanded, the dancer intoned his apology from center stage, with microphone, as the entire cast and crew watched from the theatre seats and the wings. "That's not good enough," the producer menaced through his own mike after the dancer concluded. "Tell me more."

Silence was not enough to survive in Las Vegas. I learned I must be present only on demand, a piece of motile clay submissive and infinitely malleable in the hands of the producer, a man whose name on the outdoor marquee grew progressively larger as the weeks of rehearsal passed. We were mere lights in the producer's constellation; how dare one star shine more brightly than another without his direction.

I do not sing these days, more than twenty years into my after-dancing life, but nor am I anymore mute. A turning point came one afternoon some years ago on my drive home from the university. The vanload of college boys that pulled up next to me at the stop signal looked like trouble, but noting the official insignia on the side of the van and wishing to be a good host and dutiful college employee, I rolled down my window to provide the directions these visitors from another university requested.

Pandora's box exploded and in raucous amusement these boys spewed at me a vile tempest. They knew me, they shrieked. I was a prostitute from a whorehouse in Juarez, they cackled from the safety of their car. They said they knew the way long black hairs grew on my breasts around the nipples. Shocked and shaken by their profanities, I rolled up the window to shut out the torrent and waited to escape when the light turned green.

I resisted the urge to race from the light and instead allowed the van to pass me by. I jotted down the license plate number. I scribbled their words on a scrap of paper. I called the police when I arrived home.

Though the police were impotent in responding to the verbal assault I had endured during my drive home, my husband—my hero—was not. Though he did not understand my emotions, he knew I had been deeply wounded by the words of those young men. He figured they were on campus for a sporting event, so while I went in to work that Saturday to take my mind off the previous day's incident, he began his investigation.

He called me later that morning with the information he had gathered. He had learned that the boys were members of a golf team participating in a weekend tournament. He'd spoken to their coach. He asked if I would like to join him when he went over to talk to the team after they finished their round.

We gathered at three o'clock under one of the few trees between the eighteenth hole on the golf course and the dusty parking lot: me, my husband, the coaches of host and visiting golf teams, the young men themselves and several of their parents. Their coach spoke first, expressing his dismay about the actions of the golfers the previous day, about the hours they'd been gone and the miles they'd clocked on the van when they'd been sent on a twenty-minute errand to fetch carry-out for the group. My husband spoke next, about how one day they would have wives whom they loved deeply and would want others to treat with the respect that women deserve.

My voice was forged in the fire that destroyed the MGM Grand Hotel and left me, alone and suddenly unemployed, leaving Las Vegas with the knowledge my career was in ashes and I should find for myself some new future. Getting the job had been a dream fulfilled: I showed myself and my father I had the talent to perform professionally and could make it on my own. In losing the job—even to disaster—I lost a piece of my soul.

A letter arrived months later when rehearsals were about to resume and as reconstruction neared completion. An odd twist of fate meant that I had a power the producer then lacked. Apparently, my contract gave me the option to return if I so wished, and it was up to me to release them if I did not.

I cried as I read the letter that promised I could resume my ride on the roller coaster. I could return to the glitter of Las Vegas and the glamour of performing in a multi-million dollar extravaganza—and if the way he had treated other dancers in the corps was any measure, certain persecution by the producer. I walked alone that night down the quiet streets of my desert home, tears streaming down my face as I confronted my choices: to live my dream and the nightmare it encompassed or to care for myself and let all that I'd ever wanted go.

At nineteen, I'd been one of the youngest members of the cast. I'd just turned twenty when I gathered my courage and quietly sent the contract back, registered mail, c.o.d.

I spoke, using not my words but theirs. I wanted the coach to know I was not some hysterical female upset by some mild cursing. I wanted their parents to know how well they'd raised their sons. I wanted them to remember my name, and I gave them back their words though each syllable fouled my tongue.

I lowered my eyes after reading the last line. My husband took my hand. The coach spoke again. Though the team had been winning, they would be heading home that night, having withdrawn from the tournament in disgrace. "Bitch," seethed one of the young men as he headed toward the van. "I'm sorry," said another as the group dispersed.

Today I set pen to paper and write: I have a voice. I will be heard.

2

VAGINA

To say that I have a conflicted relationship with the penis would be understatement.

Mother sometimes spoke of her own childhood awareness that boys had something girls did not. Mom envied what little boys had that little girls lacked, but her analysis would have greatly frustrated the likes of Freud. She envied not that boys had *penises*, but rather that they had *pockets*. Boys had pockets in their clothing, so they could easily carry coins and string for playing cat's cradle and all manner of interesting objects as they explored the world. It was pocket-envy that formed my mother's early attitudes toward gender difference (and resulted in the addition of pockets to the many garments she made for me as I grew up).

It would be many years before I comprehended the peripatetic nature of the penis and its perpetual search for the secret female pocket, the vagina. My first actual exposure to the male sexual organ would have been in second grade, when my dad took his first sabbatical and we lived away from the desert in the forested mountains in the northern part of the state. That year, no doubt led by the older boys who were just beginning to feel stirrings of sexual curiosity, a group of neighborhood kids formed a nudist colony that held clandestine meetings at a quiet pool created by a beaver dam at a small stream in the nearby woods. I suspect I also would have frustrated Freud because, quite frankly, I can't remember a single penis although a good number of them must have been on view. Instead, what I remember most was how cold the water felt when we stepped barefoot into the shaded pool, how beautiful our surroundings were, and how natural it felt to frolic naked in the forest, even though we knew our parents would not have approved and so we kept our adventures a solemn secret.

My next encounter, so to speak, was a year or two later at the home of a playmate, who tucked her two-year-old brother's tennis shoe at an odd angle inside her shorts then climbed on top of me in the relative privacy of her lower berth bunk bed and proceeded to pump away at my fully clothed pelvis while she related to me the details of the sexual act. This exercise left me puzzled: why in the world would anyone wish to bump pelvises when it was so much more fun to ride bikes or play hide-and-seek? I was much more intrigued when, instructed to bathe before dinner, she pointed out the stimulating possibilities of a stream of running water and certain positioning in the bathtub. We played together only that one time. I didn't want to know about the source of my playmate's precocious knowledge, and somehow I felt guilty about learning the secret delights of hydrotherapy.

It would be nice if I could relate that my introduction to the real Mr. Wiggly, that masculine dowsing rod that's always seeking the next well, occurred in the context of a romantic interlude with my first true love. That did happen—sort of—but it's not what happened next.

I had observed among my teen-aged friends that in males, adolescence apparently involves the descent of higher consciousness and cognitive function into the penis. I had supposed that this was a temporary state and had assumed that during maturation, cognitive functions in the adult male would return to the cranial cavity. I was, therefore, unprepared to learn that in some men, when cognitive function descends into the organ of engorgement during adolescence, it does so never again to emerge. I was witness to this sad and pitiful truth over and over again at work, beginning with my first job at a family-owned tourist trap restaurant where I was hired as a hostess. Within weeks, the manager was making crude jokes and suggestive remarks, which I ignored or deflected with smart responses. It was harder to ignore the uninvited touching: "Sit down and let's talk about the first thing that *comes up*," he'd leer as he'd grab my hips and pull me onto his lap behind the hostess station. He'd rub my shoulders and run his hands along my neck, sometimes kissing the nape before letting me go, in spite of the customers (who must have observed my struggles to stand and greet them) and his wife (who did the books for the restaurant in an adjoining office). He later offered me money and tried to entice me into being his mistress with a gift of jewelry (note to would-be Catholic adulterers: a 14-karat gold crucifix necklace offered to one's intended paramour sends a mixed message).

Thus began my earnest confusion about the role of the penis and the vagina in civil society. Surely, like the vagina, a penis in the workplace should be unassuming, tucked neatly away in crisply pressed khakis. The penis-at-work should peek out primly only when proper functioning of the kidneys demands. However, that boss—and several others who followed—seemed to think that Mr. Wiggly was the life of the party and the party began at work.

While I learned to avoid that employer's overtures with some success, I grew weary of the groping gauntlet it seems the possessor of a vagina must often run. For a time, I was grateful for the free treatments provided by a chiropractor as one of my employee benefits, but gradually I tired of the "good morning" and "good evening" body hugs he demanded at the beginning and end of the work day. Eventually, I began to wonder if he got more out of my adjustments than I did.

Determined to address my growing discomfort, I began by suggesting an alternative to the full frontal contact daily greetings. I screwed up my courage and extended my hand one morning, asking simply, "How about a friendly handshake?" All seemed well, though I thought it odd when he asked that I come in to work the next Saturday, when the business was closed. I wasn't even nervous as I entered his office and took a seat. He reached across the desk and handed me a small envelope, the same kind he used to deliver our paychecks and send appointment reminders to patients. "Chiropractic: The Natural Healing Art" was written across the top. Inside, he'd enclosed a check with a short, handwritten note:

Katherine,

As per paragraph 3 section D in your contract, you are being released upon written notice, because it is deemed that you are not fulfilling your duties.

He then returned to me my employment contract along with a list of his complaints about my work. I was momentarily puzzled by his actions, as he had never raised any complaints in the two months I'd been in training and under his employ, and I'd received only glowing reviews during the years I'd worked for another doctor. But the litany was brief, petty, and revealing: I'd not brought patients back to the treatment room *correctly*, which he said made patients feel uncomfortable. I'd put a patient in the wrong room and the case folder in the wrong slot on the door. I'd read personal material at work. I'd used the telephone for personal purposes. Listed last was undoubtedly the most serious offense: "Leaving immediately at lunch and the end of the day—makes me feel that you can't wait to get away from the office."

Convinced that I was in the right, I consulted the phone book and began making calls the following Monday. A representative at the state Labor and Industrial Commission said I could file a report with the Human Rights Commission, but she indicated that I needed to obtain a corroborative statement; however, I doubted that the other employee, the doctor's daughter, would be of any help. I learned that in my state, an employer did not have to give any reason or notice for termination, and that the Equal Employment Opportunity Commission (EEOC) only handled complaints against companies with fifteen or more employees.

A representative from the Commission on the Status of Women was sympathetic. "It's illegal," she remarked after I told my tale. She also referred me to the Human Rights Commission (which still needed a corroborating statement), suggested I see a counselor, and sent me an information pamphlet with the encouraging message that "despite company policies, government regulations and court precedents, fighting harassment is not easy." My case would undoubtedly end up as a he-said, she-said argument, and she indicated that a satisfactory outcome was highly unlikely.

Enough was enough: the next time Mr. Wiggly reared his pointy head at me at work, I would nip the problem in the bud, long before suggestive compliments became demands for sexual favors, before incidental touches became unquestionable gropes, and before my conscience became unsettled with doubt and guilt and thoughts that somehow I deserved the treatment I received. If need be, in the future I would treat the offending organ as an emergency brake, and give it such a yank that my firm and decisive *no* would be unmistakable in its meaning.

I had the opportunity to test my convictions after completing my master's degree and securing my first professional position as a staff member on the campus where my mother and father had both worked until they retired. I knew better than to believe that long acquaintance with people made me safe (I learned that when my best friend's father—who had recommended me for that first job at the restaurant—propositioned me in college). I had hoped I might be left simply to do my job in a large organization subject to EEOC guidelines, where the mission was to develop the mind, and where, presumably, members of the university community aspired to high ideals.

Of all places where one might entertain the possibility of enjoying a vagina-safe workplace, a university campus should never be considered one of them. College campuses can be hotbeds of illicit sexual activity: among students; among faculty and staff; and among students, faculty, and staff. My own parents met at a college football game when my aunt, a former high school classmate of Dad's, arranged to sneak her younger sister into the game at the gate Dad was working. Dad looked the other way when it was time for the high school girl to show a college ID, waiving her in though only college students with a valid ID were permitted. Their romance blossomed the next year, when Mom was a first-semester freshman and Dad, a graduate student and her math instructor. They observed a certain careful propriety during their courtship, which involved long walks around town, short drives to church, a wedding in late January, and the birth of a baby boy in the second year of their marriage. The same, however, cannot be said for all such interactions.

My own experience is a case in point. I, too, first fell in love on a university campus with an older man. He was a college student and I was still in high school. He was the partner my dance teacher chose for my first pas de deux, a coupling that lasted one evening far too late.

"What do you expect when you come to a guy's dorm room?" he said as I gathered my things and walked out the door.

If he truly loved me as I loved him, I thought, he would have listened when I said *no*. Yet after that night, as regular intercourse became a requirement for continuing our relationship, I began to see things the way he argued his point: If I truly loved him, I would allow his advances whenever he asked despite my discomfort.

The good news is that though his instrument was remarkable (the cause of comment from the back row of the theatre when he sauntered on stage in tights), his was not the weaponized penis of today, a piston capable of a four-hour erection and brutal damage to the soft, sensitive flesh of a woman's vagina if she is not properly lubricated. Nor was the drug that held me captive some date rape concoction that left me passive and forgetful. He was tender though insistent in his embrace; I complied with his wishes because I loved him, and hoped that some day he might come to love me the same way. The bad news is that one woman was not nearly enough to satisfy his prodigious sexual appetite. He made it clear to me from the start that there would be no ties in our relationship and he was honest with me about the other women, and eventually, about the other men with whom he lay.

I sought advice from the campus EEOC officer the moment the director crossed the line, when he bent down and kissed the top of my head as I worked at my desk and asked why he hadn't gotten any hugs that day. Before then, I'd interpreted his comments on my appearance and the side-by-side hugs he initiated as paternal. I had grown up on campus, his wife knew my mom from the faculty wives' book club, and, as an amateur thespian, he had been in plays with my sister and several friends. Initially, I also ignored his lewd remarks, as such colorful repartee was fairly common among the actors and dancers I had known. But when the comments grew more personal—he'd like to nibble on my cherry earrings, he'd like to know what turned me on, he aspired to be my lover—I began to take them personally and to take notes about exactly what happened and who was present, just in case the behavior escalated. I had lots of documentation, then, when I met with the EEOC officer and felt confident that with the right approach it would be possible to resolve the matter and resume what had formerly been a congenial working relationship.

To my surprise, I was told I had no choice but to file a formal, written complaint if I wanted any response. Although the campus policy on sexual harassment stated that I would be offered alternatives if I chose to remain anonymous, the only real outcome of an informal complaint would be a note in the EEOC officer's file. University policy tied the officer's hands: she was unable to act quietly on my behalf and keep my identity secret. So I filed my grievance, a two-and-one-half page, single-spaced memo with dates, direct quotes, and witnesses all named, and I added to the grievance a request for a lateral transfer within the university.

I received a response within a week. The certified letter thanked me for reporting the matter and related the outcome:

Based on the documentation reviewed, there is undisputed testimony to support allegations of perceived sexual harassment during working hours. The director's rationale that he did not intend to offend you ... does not absolve him of engaging in inappropriate behavior. Therefore, a disciplinary action memorandum has been administratively issued to him with a copy forwarded to his Personnel file.

The envelope also included a copy of the director's written response to my complaint, a document that contained no surprises. I misunderstood his intent as, *of course*, he would never do anything that would harm me or his relationship with my parents. Though policy decreed he should know his accuser, in this bureaucratic process, he would never have to face me. There would be no confrontation, no conversation, no apology. And since, as I soon learned, university policy made no accommodations for lateral transfers among professional staff, there was nothing left to do but to try to put it all behind me.

Ultimately, I resigned after a year of subtle retaliation that compromised my ability to do my job as information officer for the organization. The director decided to write and distribute press releases himself; he reassigned high-profile assignments to others after I'd done the initial legwork; during a controversial reorganization, he added another management layer between me and the department heads with whom I needed contact to prepare the organization's newsletter. I quit some time after the suicide of another staff member, and wrote a letter to the Vice President of the university articulating my concerns about morale in the organization—having been admitted to the club of those on the director's "D" list, I'd become aware of just how egregious and widespread his misbehavior had been. I added that, although I had no intention of pursuing legal action, I believed the director had retaliated against me for the grievance I'd filed and that for this reason, I was leaving my position to pursue a doctoral degree on campus.

At last I felt my words had had some small effect. Shortly after I sent my letter, I heard the director would be retiring in the coming year. Of course, he'd be honored for his achievements and allowed the golden parachute many administrators enjoy, an opportunity to teach part time for up to three years. His choice? He opted to teach in the department where I was pursuing my Ph.D. I'd quit my job to get away from that man, yet there I was: screwed again.

My observation is that the penis and the vagina are central to two main lessons popular culture teaches. The Rule of the Penis is that *Men gain sex through power.* The source of that power—physical, financial, emotional—doesn't really matter. If a man has command of one of these sources, his penis can be satisfied.

The corollary to that rule—The Rule of the Vagina—is this: *Women gain power through sex.* Maybe it's because enough women have bought into this kind of thinking that intercourse has become a kind of contemporary pelvic handshake among new acquaintances. Believing women gain power through sex is convenient if you happen to be a man with a dipstick aching to take the plunge. I just don't buy it. If this were true, then innocent men would have lobbied the EEOC long ago for protection from the unwelcome advances of predatory women.

Perhaps it's time for the EEOP, the Equal Exposure Opportunity Penis: a penis portrayed in books and films and the nightly news in the same way women's breasts are, a penis revealed in the lines of tight-fitting pants and subject to wardrobe malfunctions during the Super Bowl. A penis supported by an underwire jockstrap worn by scantily clad men at Hooters. If we showed the penis in all its variety—the shy turtle penis that ducks and hides from a bath of cold water, the flaccid penis that flops around when a man moves or walks—we wouldn't have to rely on Oprah and that scientific study she quoted to learn that Caucasian men are merely middling when it comes to the average size of the appendage.

If we had the EEOP, we might not then be as surprised as the elderly couple I overheard in an upscale restaurant relating to their senior citizen friends their experiences on a nudie beach. One man had a shock of white hair, a long bulbous nose on a ruddy face, and small beady eyes that twinkled as he spoke. "We went to a nude beach in St. Martin's thinking we'd see something good," he said. "The first person we saw was a seventy-year-old man out to here," and he gestured a belly that was even rounder than his own. At which point his neatly manicured wife laughed and rolled her eyes in unison with her words, "It went downhill from there."

The vagina is neither an essential way station on the road to success nor the key that locks up a man's heart, yet believing this is so contributes nicely to a program of male sexual conquest. The penis simply doesn't belong in action at work, and intimate relations in a healthy relationship involve much more than penile thumping in a compliant vagina. In fact, one do-it-yourself guide explains seven dimensions of sexual intimacy. "It's very complicated," my husband once remarked, "In all my years studying physics.... I mean, Einstein needed only four dimensions to describe the universe."

3

WOMB

Likening monthly menstrual onslaught to visits from a kind of twisted Santa bearing a little red surprise, my high school gym-slash-sex-education teacher announced the first day of class, "There's no such thing as cramps." To our groans of protest at this pronouncement, this same woman also told tales of an unwed teen who won a track meet in the a.m. and to everyone's surprise birthed a baby in the p.m. As labor was fictitious to my gym teacher, it was no surprise to learn that dysmenorrhea was as well: she was clearly one of the 60 percent of all women for whom periods are a nuisance but not a pain. For the remaining 40 percent of the menstruating population, each month's flow is accompanied by myriad physical and emotional discomforts. For fully 10 percent, those "discomforts" are debilitating. Unfortunately, I was twenty years and a two-second Google search away from being able to disabuse her of her fallacious notions and inform her of the facts, so I said nothing and suited up.

When I later fainted after an emergency visit to the restroom during chorus, the time came to confront the symptoms of what ailed me, symptoms that my gym teacher would have attributed to an overactive imagination. My periods were marked by abdominal pain so severe that on those nights of onset I gave up my bed for the bathroom floor as I could not leave the toilet for fear of soiling my bedclothes with vomit, blood, or feces. My midsection wrung itself intermittently for hours on end, sometimes succeeding in repeated simultaneous evacuation from multiple orifices—while diarrhea and blood issued into the stool, I wretched and emptied the contents of my stomach into the wastepaper basket. When each episode passed, I would clean myself and cry as I brushed my teeth, trying to rinse the awful taste of bile out of my mouth. Then I'd lay down curled in fetal position around the commode, grateful for the cool comfort of the tile floor and the warmth of a hot water bottle held close to my belly, hoping for some moments of sleep before the next wave began.

That particular day, my sight began to blacken as I left the restroom. Horrified by the possibility that the fainting spell that sometimes marked the beginning of my cycle could afflict me on the school grounds, I reached for the wall to control my fall as my knees crumpled. I heard the cholos nearby laugh, hooting, "Hey man, do you think we should save her life?" In stubborn refusal of their mocking charity, I struggled to revive myself and stumbled blindly back to the classroom where I finally collapsed, only to be paraded down the halls a short while later to the nurse's office in a wheelchair, moaning and crying uncontrollably, my knees huddled to my chest in a desperate effort to find physical comfort.

Though the pain eventually subsided, the nightmare continued with my first visit to my mother's Catholic gynecologist, who advised me that having a baby was the surefire cure for whatever ailed me. What kind of advice is that to give to a sixteen-year-old virgin who had yet to enjoy a lover's caress? The doctor then prescribed that my cervix be cauterized to correct what he deemed a birth defect—to close up a small area of flesh that wasn't quite completely formed. He thought perhaps I'd been a premie, but my nearly obsessive habit for punctuality began with my birth, on exactly the date predicted.

A week or so later I lost my virginity to a machine. The wonders of automation meant no doctor need be present for cervical cauterization: once my feet were in stirrups and the nurse had plugged the cryosurgery unit into my vagina, I was left alone in the examining room to contemplate the joys of motherhood and the humor in obstetrics as illustrated in cartoons and posters on the ceiling. If the purpose of this procedure was to ease my menstrual discomfort, it failed miserably. Though I experienced no physical pain during the procedure itself, by the time we arrived home I was doubled over again and begging my mother to *please* run out and purchase whatever drug it was the doctor had said might help. Successive cycles were little different than before.

For all the fuss and furor of its onset, my flow has always been disproportionately mild. I envied my friends, some of whom had such low body weight that their periods stopped altogether and others who reported needing both ultra heavy duty napkins plus tampons the size of Texas to dam their fecund reservoirs. While my friends might suffer the embarrassment of an unannounced crimson tide, my cramps gave me ample warning of the impending trickle; for me, several panty liners would just about do the job for the two-to-three days of my monthly bleeding. When later in life my husband and I were unable to conceive, I grieved that each month my body should cry wolf so loudly and then cheat me of its natural reward.

So I rebelled against the tyranny of the moon and refused to track the tide. I considered gynecologists the "dentists of the other end." I joked half-seriously about cosmetic hysterectomy. I eagerly awaited menopause. When the happy day finally arrived that my perimenopausal symptoms caused me to suspect my periods were at last coming to an end, I began to jot little red symbols on the calendar to mark the days I bled. To my dismay, I discovered that I was as regular as clockwork.

Within the year, though, things began to change and the clock went a little haywire. After six weeks of bloating and cramps marked by two periods—one at week four and the other at week six—I finally succumbed to the marketing temptations of a menopause monitoring product to discover just how far along I was. I learned from the handy chart enclosed in the package that the sequence of two tests could tell me precisely where I was in the two-to-ten years of the climacteric: that I was approaching perimenopause (two negatives), that I was experiencing perimenopause (positive and negative), or that I was actually near menopause (two positives). The trick was going to be in taking the test itself, which to my surprise required following the same procedure women follow to determine if they are pregnant. My task was to capture my first morning pee in a small plastic cup, moisten a test stick with the urine for exactly five seconds, and wait exactly twenty minutes for the test stick to ripen so I could read the results immediately thereafter. Therein lies the rub.

Somewhere between Pampers, tampons, and Depends lie the brief undiapered phases of a woman's life. We are little prepared to appreciate the freedom of the longest phase, between potty training and puberty, when a pair of panties and your personal self-control are all the protection needed to have a clean and dry day. And while I expected that with puberty my freedom from sanitary embarrassment would wane with the onset of menstruation, I have been little prepared for the loss in bladder control that often results in an urge to purge that awakens me each morning at four thirty. It's hard enough to make it to the toilet in time when your brain has decided to dream you a handy commode where you sit struggling for relief in confused frustration until some corner of consciousness stirs you from the bed. Requiring that you find your glasses and the necessary supplies, hit that tiny plastic cup with a stream of pee, open the hermetically sealed sterile package so you can dip the pee-pee stick in the cup, follow precise timing requirements, and stay awake for another twenty minutes is just too much to ask.

It turns out that such nocturnal interruptions are relatively common among women. Nearly a third of women between ages thirty to forty-nine have occasional episodes of leaky pee or *urinary incontinence*, particularly during and after pregnancy. So do over half of women ages forty-five to fifty. The frequency of such episodes often increases as our estrogen levels decline and the muscles of the pelvic floor, which support our abdominal organs, begin to weaken. *Stress urinary incontinence* occurs when we laugh, cough, or move in certain ways and feel a trickle of tinkle between the thighs. Often attributed to an overactive or irritated bladder, anxiety may also contribute to *urge incontinence,* such as my early awakenings and the strong need to relieve myself I've always felt before any sort of public performance.

Given my personal history, I imagine there's good reason my bladder might be irritated with me. Having once consumed forty-four ounce, super-sized tubs of di[ur]et[ic] cola with reckless abandon, it's no wonder that my bladder has begun to exact its revenge by acting as if it has shrunk to the size of a thimble. Like other desert-dwelling females, I learned at a very young age to acquire a certain bladder agility because vacation travel out west means covering long distances with few towns and fewer rest stops, many of which lack "facilities." I'm convinced that even the most refined and tenderfooted city dweller would develop entirely new standards after one experience with a "no-pee town"—a town where a sign on the door of the only public establishment proclaims there's NO PUBLIC TOILET—when your only recourse is a desperate drive to the nearest national park or monument where you're at last able to relieve yourself after the hordes of Harleys have vacated the area.

A basic repertoire of the desert-traveler's sanitary survival skills involves *metered sipping, speed peeing, peeing on demand,* and *two-door peeing* (possible only when traveling in a four-door sedan or its equivalent). Otherwise, you're faced with two grim alternatives: Competing with a rattler for the scanty privacy offered by a scraggly bush, or using the dreaded pee-pee cup, a portable urinal that is woefully unresponsive to logistical wrangling in the back seat of a car or to sudden bumps, swerves, and stops when somebody else is driving. (No comment about that time I turned up the radio and crawled from the front seat to the back seat ostensibly to search for something, but in truth to pee surreptitiously into my soft drink cup because the hubby thought it was too soon to stop.)

Catastrophe cannot be prevented by even the most intimate knowledge of all the roadside stops and exactly how many ounces of a favorite soft drink one can consume before arriving: lines at the ladies' at a rustic two-holer can cause real problems. I still recall with some horror one occasion when I heard the approach of heavy footsteps just as I was entering the final drip-zip-and-go phase of a surreptitious visit to the men's side of a desert rest stop. Moments later, a hairy hand reached up and gripped the top of the privacy wall separating the urinal from the stall I occupied. I held my breath as I heard a heavy sigh and the swish of a steady stream as fervent as my own had been just moments before. Time stopped and my mind raced. I'd asked my sister to watch the door—why hadn't she warned off intruders until I emerged? Should I try to make plopping and dripping sounds to justify my continued presence in the stall? Were other men waiting and *did they need to poop*? While I eventually escaped the men's room unnoticed, embarrassed only by my accidental role as a potty *auditeur*, I vowed to introduce more discipline into my personal strategic peeing practices.

Indeed, discipline is an important quality to develop as one resolves to eliminate unplanned elimination. A mere two hundred to three hundred repetitions a day of Kegel exercises can strengthen the pubococcygeal (or PC) muscle, eliminate pee-pee problems, and—as a side benefit—put a smile on the face of one's [hetero]sexual partner. Don't be confused by the name: a regular dash to the nearest Swedish pastry shop won't generate the same happy results. These mysterious and satisfying exercises were named for their originator, Dr. Arnold Kegel. Since science tells us that most women cannot locate and contract the PC muscle by verbal instruction alone (I'd love to see Dr. Kegel's research notes on this), you will be reassured to learn that the captains of industry have been hard at work devising a dizzying array of technologies we can use to better achieve our aim.

These devices are referred to by the amusing misnomer, "Kegel exercisers," implying a category of equipment used to exercise one's Kegel. (Any questions about why verbal instructions might be confusing?) In evaluating the various options, I have discerned some significant differences among them. Several rather frightening devices—one held between the thighs and two variations to be inserted—reminded me of spring-action salad tongs. They each had two surfaces connected at one end and a sturdy coil creating tension between the two lengths of plastic.

More common is what I call the "vaginal barbell": smooth, steel rods with bulbous ends. These range in length from two and one-half inches to seven inches. Some are curved and have a coated surface, looking rather like a man's—well, you know what. In online testimonials, one happy user reported "wearing" one of the heavy rods while she vacuumed and enjoying excellent results.

And if neither pubic salad tongs nor vaginal barbells appeal, you can always get a "personal trainer," a small electronic monitor connected to an inflatable "vaginal sensor." The personal trainer measures pressure on the sensor created when a woman contracts the PC muscle and (no surprises here) registers on the display a series of concentric smiles that increase in size and number with the strength of the contraction.

At the moment, my own problems with incontinence are relatively minor—I'd like to be able to hit that damned early morning pee cup to find out when my *meno* will actually *pause* or manage an extra gulp or two of water before my exercise class without requiring a trip to the ladies' halfway through (there's a reason they call it "Pee-lot-ease"). Just as reducing the size and frequency and caffeine content of my travel beverages would have reduced my urgent need for carefully timed rest stops, I rather think that my early morning urges could be curbed by eliminating the evening cup of chamomile tea that my doctor recommended to help me sleep.

4

BREASTS

There are two small reasons I don't usually tell people about my experiences as a performer in Las Vegas—one is on the right side of my chest, and the other is on the left. Mention "Vegas" to those of a certain generation and the eyes suddenly flick south of the face and cloud with images of a multitude of mesmerizing mammaries. In polite company, immediate explanation must follow, sounding lame despite the truth: I auditioned as a *covered dancer*, one of several roles that allowed for a certain modesty, as my grandfather planned to join me at Christmas to see the show after it opened. Even if I'd been interested, at just under five foot seven I was technically too short to be in the show (five foot eight was the advertised minimum), barely tall enough to be considered for a small corps of "pony" dancers, and altogether too short to be topless. Given the enormity of the stage—half a football field and several stories high—there's apparently a problem with perspective if one's breasts are too close to the ground.

During the audition, when the producer wanted to find out who among us in this cattle call planned to try out for the higher-paying topless roles, he asked first for a show of hands—and then for a show of nipples. "Let's see 'em," he barked when the dancers hesitated. While the men and we coupleds stepped to the side of the stage, the remaining women stripped to the waist and began to dance.

An old boyfriend, an artist accustomed to working with live models, once remarked comfortingly to me that the size and shape of the human breast was greatly exaggerated. Until that moment and despite plenty of locker room experience, I had no idea of the truth of his words. Even photos in *National Geographic* had not prepared me for the impending display of breasts so unlike in shape and size from the careful selection that would ultimately appear in the show like so many plump peaches on display. There were surgically standardized Barbie breasts punctuated by barely perceptible nipples and snowy mounds with *stage nipples,* prominent tips that would show from front row to the last seat in the balcony. I tried not to gawk at the sight of mismatched mosquito bites, ski slope breasts, and pendulous orbs that followed a dancer's body a half beat behind as she moved. For the producer, choosing breasts was a serious task. He needed perfectly matched pairs and had to consider as a business risk the eventual effect of gravity.

As for myself, after that day I felt a lot less concerned about the "problems" with my breasts, which were readily solved by costuming alterations specified by the world-renowned designer for the show, Bob Mackie. My costume-fitting experience with him was markedly different from the one for "Dying Swan," in my home town several years earlier. I'd stripped and slipped into the creamy white tutu when my Dutch ballet teacher cackled in her thick accent as she marked the alterations, "Kaaa-taaa-reeen! You rrreeeally haf no boobies!" I molted right then and there.

In terms of mammary variety, I expect Mr. Mackie had at least the experience of the average physician (and perhaps the average gynecologist) as he carried out his craft with detachment. After all, the Utah dance teacher who first told us about the jobs in Vegas said that, sure, for the first few minutes the breasts are all you see in a Las Vegas spectacle, but boredom eventually sets in and you start to look for something interesting. I was grateful that during the fitting Mr. Mackie was subtle and disinterested and merely made note that my costumes would require additional anterior padding to augment what nature had given me (don't believe what you think you see in Vegas, because even the bust pads have false nipples).

Our culture is obsessed with the perfect breast, the peak upon which the city of Las Vegas was built. Yet perfection, to Mother Nature, has little to do with the teat as a means of titillation. Even the "perfect" set granted by Mother Nature will change over time as she intended, becoming richly abundant upon childbearing and reducing her stores when fertility wanes.

During the audition, I came closest to revealing my own twin peaks beyond what is revealed by a dancer's normally scant attire when the producer announced that the rest of us needed to bring teeny bikinis the next day so our bodies could be checked for unsightly marks or scars that would disqualify us from consideration for the cast. Having survived a somewhat accident-prone childhood, I felt lucky to be able to pass this test.

Mother guesses that I was three or four years old when I climbed to the seat of our yellow kitchen stepstool to "help" her fry tostadas for one of the many faculty parties we hosted at our house. I wanted to watch as Mom placed the soft corn triangles in the electric skillet where they bubbled fragrantly, and then later scooped the crisp, tasty chips onto layers of paper toweling to drain and cool. I didn't notice as I climbed the steps to my favorite perch that the old stool wobbled precariously; moments later, as I turned and shifted my body on the seat, the stool suddenly collapsed. I reached forward reflexively, grasping for anything that would help to break my fall. The smooth, aluminum sides of the countertop offered no purchase, so I grasped the only other available surface, the side walls of the electric skillet. Chair, skillet, oil, child: we slipped and clattered to the floor.

Mother quickly swept me up, stripped me, and doused me with cool water in the bathtub while Daddy grabbed the car keys and told the party guests what had happened. He must have asked someone to look after my brother while we headed to the emergency room, then rushed outside to start the car. Mother pulled me from the tub, wrapped me loosely in a clean towel and carried me outside, holding me gingerly in her arms as we sped toward the hospital. A white-coated man pulled sterile gauze soaked with a sickly yellow ointment from stainless steel basins and wrapped first my hands and arms and then my belly from armpits to waist. Though I was able to go home to heal, the intervening weeks were filled with other small horrors: a return to the helplessness of an infant and teasing from my brother who called me "baby" and "the mummy"; a bloodied spot in my left armpit caused when the doctor inadvertently pulled off a small patch of skin when changing my bandages; the sterilized needle Dad used to pop the blisters that covered my knuckles and palms once my hands were finally freed from the gauze bindings.

The day that I was burned, Mother's quick actions made a significant difference in the severity of my injuries and my ability to heal with virtually no scars. Just as a hard-boiled egg continues to cook although it has been removed from the heat, flesh, once heated to burning, also continues to "cook" until cooled. Had she acted according to common folk remedies—covering my wounds with butter or ointment—she might have made things worse because oils and salves can lock in heat, driving damage deeper into the skin. By running cool water over my burns, she was able to quickly stop the cooking of my flesh, just like quickly blanching an egg in cold water after boiling helps keep the surface of the yolk from turning a sickly gray-green.

BLAST HURTS THREE, the headline read. A powerful explosion jolted one wall six inches off its foundation. Smoke and flames spread throughout the small house, including three of the bedrooms. News of the blast rocked our home though the calamity occurred fifteen miles away in a small rural village south of the city.

I'd spent the night in one of those bedrooms with my best friend, Terrie, just six months earlier, after the front page of the local paper had announced SMALL GIRL ELECTROCUTED IN ACCIDENT. Terrie and I met after our moms shared a room in the maternity ward two years earlier, when Mrs. Barnett had Tim and Mom had Liz. Mrs. Barnett also had a daughter, just my age. There were no other little girls near their rural home, so despite the distance between our houses, every now and then Terrie Barnett and I got together to play.

The accounts in the papers didn't say much—the cause of the explosion was unknown and being investigated. Mr. Barnett escaped without injury and two-year-old Tim had slight burns and was essentially ok. But Terrie had second and third degree burns on her feet and on her beautiful face. The papers stated also that Mrs. Barnett had second and third degree burns but didn't say where, only commenting that her condition was guarded.

I clipped the news items and thought of my overnight stay six months earlier. When my sister died and Mother asked if I'd like to attend the funeral, I'd said I wanted to be with my best friend instead.

My brother's right hand has a round scar about the size of a half dollar where skin from one leg was grafted in place to cover a deep hole from pavement burns worn in his flesh as he skidded along a stretch of asphalt after being thrown from his motorcycle. His gifted hands—hands that painted landscapes, played the violin, built models, and fixed motorcycles—bore wounds that had until now left no visible marks. The deeper damage was done years before when Mother sent Mike to look for my sister Amy, who had been unusually quiet for far too long.

Michael reached for her to pull her out of the water. He touched her cheek but quickly recoiled, shocked by the current still flowing through her tiny frame. So he grasped for something dry—the sunshine of the brightly colored fabric or perhaps the decorative buttons at her shoulders, three small green globes Mother had stitched to the matching copy of my favorite dress that Amy was wearing. Then he ran into the house screaming "Amy's dead! Amy's dead!"

Mother knelt at Amy's side, doing her best with cardio-pulmonary resuscitation, but there was nothing she could do for little Amy. And there was nothing she could do for my brother, who had installed the bare wire that Amy had backed into as part of one of his inventions, not knowing that a short inside the window air conditioner it touched would make the ground wire live and our sister dead.

The papers did not say, but I later heard that Mrs. Barnett ran through a wall of flames to rescue her son Tim, holding him closely to her breast, sheltering his small body with her own. Her nylon nightgown melted to her skin, leaving little that could be used later for grafts that might have saved her life. Just a few months earlier I'd asked her why my sister had died. She paused before answering, resting the laundry hamper on her hip and gazing out the window, her face golden with sunlight. She placed the hamper on the washer, turned, and with gentle hands, smoothed my tousled hair and wiped the tears from my cheeks. "Sometimes children are so precious," she lovingly replied, "God picks them for his flower basket."

5

SKIN

Hidden from sight within the walls of the Deli of the MGM Grand Hotel, two small copper wires made contact, first overheating until they glowed white hot, then arcing, sparking, and ultimately igniting the surrounding building materials. The fire was discovered shortly after seven in the morning on November 21, 1980, when, thirteen minutes after it first ignited, open flames burst through the walls.

Poor installation of the wiring plus heat and vibration from the compressor/condenser on the pastry display case in the Deli had created perfect nursery conditions for the ensuing inferno. Vibrations caused the aluminum raceway that housed the wires to come into contact with an uninsulated section of the copper tubing that carried Freon to and from the display case. This resulted in galvanic action, the kind of chemical reaction that powers batteries. Over time, the aluminum raceway that shielded the wiring became corroded, exposing the two copper wires inside to heat and moisture within the walls. Air improperly vented from the compressor/condenser had over six years of near continuous operation kept the area constantly overheated, causing the insulation on the wires as well as the building materials to deteriorate, a circumstance that not only left them tinder dry but surrounded by combustible gases that responded eagerly to the first spark.

Within six minutes of discovery, the entire casino—an area larger than a football field—was engulfed in flames. The few automated sprinklers installed in the two million square-foot monolith protected several small areas of the hotel from utter destruction, but ultimately were no match for the conflagration.

Fire crews arrived quickly, but fled almost immediately after entering as an enormous fireball erupted across the ground floor and blew out the doors at the main entrance to the hotel. This exceedingly hot fire—burning at temperatures as high as +2,800° F—generated enormous pressure as the gases from combustion permeated the building, seeping through the walls and seeking escape through even the tiny gaps surrounding the shower stall plumbing in guest rooms. Inside the casino, superheated gases had quickly raised the temperature of furnishings, gaming equipment, and interior finish materials, including numerous "crystal" chandeliers made of flammable plastics as well as cellulose ceiling tiles and the twelve tons of adhesive with which they had been installed. *Flashover*—spontaneous combustion of the entire area—quickly ensued as the fire fed gluttonously on the combustible materials that had created the glittering grandeur on the ground floor of the hotel. Though fire crews ultimately contained and extinguished the blaze rapidly enough to prevent its spread throughout the high rise, eighty-five people were killed and seven hundred people were injured in one of the worst hotel fires in US history.

I escaped an uncertain fate only by virtue of a recent change in our rehearsal schedule that left me at home in bed at seven that morning instead of in the basement just beneath the casino having breakfast in the employee cafeteria at the time of the fire. I woke to a knock on my door from a neighbor who simply said, "I thought you'd want to know—your hotel's burning."

I stood barefooted on my balcony and looked to the east, where a billowing storm of black smoke choked the morning sky. Helicopters circled the hotel seeking gaps in the smothering charcoal blanket so they could rescue those people who had fled to the rooftop. Open windows hung with bed linens marked the desperate attempts of guests to escape the noxious fumes funneled skyward through the stairwells and elevator shafts of the twenty-six-story high-rise. Groggy and bewildered, I wondered if I was supposed to go in to work later that day.

I cannot imagine what my father must have felt when he first heard of the fire at the MGM Grand Hotel as he sat down to begin a bidding contest with my twelve-year-old sister Elizabeth at a bridge tournament in Dunblane, Scotland. I cannot imagine how it would feel to be confronted a second time with the loss of a daughter when out of town, this time an ocean away from home instead of a mere five-hour drive across the state. I cannot imagine how he felt the first time ten years earlier when he was told that my three-and-a-half-year-old sister, Amy, was dead, electrocuted in a freak accident that involved a short in a window air conditioner, a bare wire, and a small flood of cool water in our side yard that Amy had started when she picked up the garden hose and turned on the tap to water flowers. I cannot imagine his pain or the sense of utter helplessness and despair he might have felt, this time unable even to call to find out if I was living or dead as I had not yet had a telephone installed. But I can imagine that it was perhaps at this moment that the seemingly unbreachable wall of silence between us rose to impenetrable heights, built to protect a tender heart from further hurt as he allowed for the worst and waited for news.

Three days had passed by the time my parents learned from my brother I was safe. I imagine he'd gotten word from some other relative as jammed phone lines, unanswered calls, and my small stash of coins limited my ability to contact others from the pay phone at the apartment complex. By the time Mother sat down to write and let me know they'd received the news, I'd emptied my bank account, packed the camper shell of the pickup like a giant box, and fled Las Vegas for smalltown Colorado and shelter in my uncle's home, my compulsive need to connect with family unaverted by forecasts of a massive snowstorm that quickly blanketed the western states as I drove.

The drive should have taken less than ten hours, but shortly after I entered Utah, heavy snowfall and snowpack on the roadway forced me to reconsider my plans. I consulted the map and determined to stick it out until I reached the next tiny settlement before reluctantly stopping for the night. When I arrived, I walked inside the gas station—the only building in sight—to find a large, roughly clad family seated to eat at a picnic table, the family dog at their feet awaiting scraps. The tiny dot on the map was literally just a wide spot in the road. There were no lodgings nearby and the closest town was behind me, back toward Vegas. Blinded by tears of frustration and whiteout conditions, I sobbed uncontrollably as I turned the truck around.

How I made it to the small motel I do not know; it was still snowing and I was still crying when I entered the lobby, where I haltingly explained my circumstances and asked the proprietors if I might use a telephone. Unable to imagine stopping my journey until welcoming arms embraced me at its end, I had decided to drive some eight hundred miles back through Vegas to southern New Mexico if the roads were clearer to the south. If the way to family was blocked, I would seek solace with friends.

Devastated by news that the storm surrounded my location, I called my uncle's home and told them I would not be driving further that day. I stayed overnight in that tiny town in Utah, comforted by the kindness of strangers who trusted me to reverse the charges for the phone calls and allowed me the privacy of making them from a vacant room. The next day I prayed with each passing moment for the patience to drive safely over the miles of snowpacked highways and icy mountain roads that separated me from family.

For years, my father and I have seldom exchanged in person even a dozen heartfelt words except in anger. When I recently unearthed a small collection of letters from Scotland that I scarcely remember receiving, I was surprised to see how many were from him and how constant was his contact before I left New Mexico in late August, after I arrived in Nevada, and in the months after the fire when I'd eventually returned to New Mexico long before they returned to the States. After putting the letters in order and adjusting my glasses, I began to read.

Saturday, Aug 16, 1980

Dear Katherine,

I am writing this while waiting to call you in an hour or so. Laura and Lizzie are shopping for the remainder of Lizzie's school clothes, and I am waiting for the man who is to bring us a B+W TV set which we will rent for the next 10 months …

I was astonished to see that my father's tight, economical handwriting completely filled the front and back of three tissue-thin sheets with richly detailed descriptions of their new surroundings.

I have sketched a floor plan of our apartment below. Our flat is part of an old mansion built around the turn of the century, and typical of the architecture of the period. Wood floors, high ceilings, large windows, fireplaces with mantels, large bedrooms. (It reminds me a lot of my grandmother's house on Twelfth Street in OK City.) Closets are tiny and clothes are hung in wardrobes …

While I remembered with great frustration my father's Spartan sense of economy, that same inflexible frugality meant that no sheet of paper ever came my way unless completely filled with news about their adventures overseas.

September 17, 1980

Dear Katherine,

It was a real treat to get your letter on my birthday. We're very glad you arrived safely in Las Vegas, and are settled in. We're happy you've found nice friends …

We've done a bit of touring around in the last few weeks. We visited Scone Palace in Perth on Saturday Aug 23. This is the site of an old castle and the place where Scotland's kings were crowned on the "Stone of Scone"—stolen away to London by Edward I in 1296 …

As time passed, he penned sentimental longings for familiar scenes and events back home.

I find I miss watching the Dallas Cowboys on the tube on weekends. We do have cricket matches—that's a sport that for excitement and suspense has birdwatching as its nearest rival. And of course there's golf, and an occasional soccer match (football not "American football") and the biggie this week—international darts!

I recalled none of the wry sense of humor in his letters, their light and loving touch, and the gentle affection that they conveyed. I could see how I had been blinded then by my deep sense of failure at becoming once more financially dependent after the fire and feeling myself a most unworthy expense. Conscious only of my own pain, I had rejected my father's gentle gestures, instead inflicting wounds he must have felt deeply not just at that moment but over and again through the years as together we replayed this dysfunctional duet, one of us softened and seeking connection, and the other, consumed by hurt, thin-skinned, and refusing to be touched. I grieved as I realized I had probably placed the final brick myself—not then but years later, when I turned my father out of our home and told him when he visited, he'd have to find another place to stay. I had hoped when he stayed with us while in town to do some consulting he would join in the happiness my husband and I shared, but his idea of being a thoughtful guest was to stay out of the way as much as possible, to come and go in silence. Eventually I could no longer bear what I felt daily as rejection.

Time has altered my ability to see my father through the pages he penned during the months my family spent overseas. I find it is only now that my heart is open to the messages my father sent me half my lifetime ago. As time, geography, and politics have heightened the rough and stony barrier between us, I'm grateful to have found these small chinks in the wall, and I wait and I hope for a sign there is still life and love on the other side.

6

FEET

We called the dogs so we could put them back on lead as soon as we saw the leather-skinned stranger step towards us. Looking as if he'd walked straight out of the 1860s and into the twentieth century, he was leading a pack mule heavily laden with saddlebags, supplies, and rifle.

"Pardon me," he greeted us, "Can you tell me what day it is?"

For as long as we lived in the Southwest, our Sunday morning tradition included loading the dogs into the car and heading to the edge of town, east toward the craggy Organ Mountains or west, beyond the Rio Grande, and exploring the territory in which we lived. From the beginning, long walks—first in the desert, now in the city—have been one of the great joys of my marriage. After a belated honeymoon trip to the Rocky Mountains that included a ten-mile "warm-up" hike the first day, I was careful to label future peregrinations *walks* rather than hikes, because I learned that my husband and I define *hike* quite differently. No physical discomfort is enough to dampen my husband's child-like enthusiasm for exploring what beckons just beyond view. For me, the knee problems that ultimately forced me to give up dancing dictated how enthusiastically I ventured up a steep mountain grade, for fear that the way down would be spent scooting along on my butt. Furthermore, when I gave up toe shoes, I resolutely refused to voluntarily endure foot pain and blisters ever again.

The small crimson stain seeped from beneath the surface in disciplined rows across the smooth grain of shiny pink satin. I knew at once when I glimpsed her shoes as she smiled and flitted lithely off stage that my fellow dancer suffered a silent agony. Joint pain and blisters are common when a dancer graduates from soft ballet slippers to shiny satin toe shoes, but you know when there's enough blood to have saturated the interior of the shoe and made its way through the layers of burlap, paper, and glue, that inside the shiny casing, her feet are hamburger. Introduced in Romantic ballets some two hundred years ago, pointe work allowed females to rise ephemerally above their male counterparts in ballets that involved tragic combinations of love, death, and mysticism. Aerial wires, graceful leaps, and, as cobblers developed their craft, stiff satin prisons on the feet allowed women to inhabit the air in their roles as spiritual creatures that haunted unfaithful lovers. Though initially women rose to the tips of their toes only momentarily, so sensational was the response that today's choreography may demand a dancer to spend most of her time on stage *en pointe*, even jumping and leaping onto the tips of her toes.

The cobbler's technology granted women enduring power and priority on the stage, an authority from which they have yet to be shaken despite the charisma and brilliance of male dancers such as Nureyev, Villella, and Baryshnikov. Despite the appearance of fragility, the ballerina dominates the stage, with male partner in the background to assist. For a young girl, the price for this power is small: aches and blisters, until the skin toughens and the feet strengthen enough to withstand the punishment of unnatural poses.

Though on stage they contribute to the dancer's illusion of weightlessness, new toe shoes are both slippery because of the satin exterior and unforgivingly rigid because of the materials used to support the feet at the front of the shoe, called the *toe box*. The shoes may require extensive attention by the dancer to break them in: I learned from others how to slip the shoes between a door and the door frame near the hinges, then to use leverage from closing the door to squeeze and soften the toe box so the shoes were more flexible. Breaking them in is an art in itself, as it also shortens the life of the shoes because the same actions that eliminate discomfort also eliminate support.

The hand-made shoes are expensive, and as a student of the dance, I could ill afford the cost ballet companies absorb for dancers who'll wear out several pairs during a single evening's performance. So, I learned other tricks to prolong their short lives: to coat the insides with a particular brand of floor polish and place the shiny shoes in a warm oven to bake until the toe box hardened again into a shape molded especially to the dancer's foot. As there was no precise recipe, I learned that the trick was leaving them in just long enough to cure the acrylic in the flooring product, yet retrieving them before the satin was singed, turning an odd shade of toasted pink.

She struggled up the bleachers, placing two hands on the plank seat of the row above, then arduously followed first with one foot, then the other, and when she'd reached my row, she turned around to watch the action on the seventeenth green at the U.S. Women's Open. "I have such funny feet," she remarked to her companion after she had settled, and I shifted my gaze discreetly downward to see.

Her feet were loosely bound in the vibrant blue webbing of rugged hiking sandals. Thin white scars traced the length of each oddly-angled toe on her shrunken right foot, the nails brightly painted with fuchsia polish. By comparison, her left foot was larger, fleshy and swollen, a mismatch to the right. Her tanned skin was mottled with age spots, her gnarled fingers bedecked with animal-themed jewelry that exposed a sense of whimsy matched by the beaded ice-cream cones on her cheery white t-shirt. Her cropped hair framed a pleasing face, brightened by the warm smile she flashed as she inquired about the seat I was saving for my husband. She climbed into newly vacated seats the next row higher in the grandstand, settled, and laughed, hoping out loud that my husband wasn't so tall he'd block her view when he returned to his spot.

I wondered whether the snowy-haired woman had, like my father, con-tracted paralytic polio when she was a child. Dad's feet, too, were marked with thin scars and obvious asymmetry, his gait uneven as well, perma-nently altered by the crippling effects of the disease. I believe Dad's spirit was once as unafflicted as this woman's: Mother tells of how he learned to walk on his hands when he couldn't use his legs and feet, and how he swam to build strength and endurance as he recovered from the disease. And when his second-born child came along, a little girl with caramel curls and bright green eyes, he put music on the record player and danced with her, her face upturned and arms reaching to meet his, her tiny toes resting on his tender feet to follow the pattern of steps he made. Once, he even sang and danced on stage in a small town production of *Guys and Dolls*; I listened as Daddy practiced "Luck Be A Lady" and watched with rapt attention from the pocket-sized balcony (a dozen seats next to the light booth) in the old adobe vaudeville theatre and movie house. He might have been *chorus* in the program, but to me, he was a star. It wasn't until I grew older and heavier that I learned the one cardinal rule of our house-hold: do *not* step on Daddy's feet.

My feet have always been a source of power and strength. They kept me grounded. They held me up with little complaint. They launched me sky-ward and caught me safely when I soared. My feet *moved* me. For a former dancer, I have remarkably beautiful feet, not the gnarled and misshapen appendages one more frequently finds on those who've made a living from the art. My feet are long and slender, with only minor hints at my previous occupation, slight bunions and little toes that curl in upon themselves.

They grumbled when I encased them in toe shoes and were grateful for the change offered by the silver Capezio high heels that I wore in Vegas. Compared to toe shoes, the three-and-one-half-inch heels were like house slippers, and I thought nothing of how the miraculous architecture of the foot, though compromised by my shoes, allowed me sure-footed to leap, land, fold to the floor, then rise yet again for another sequence of steps. You have to trust your feet to find the floor, even when the costuming, choreography, and a set change spell danger. For one part of the Vegas show, my costume had a train that I worried about tripping over as I sauntered, head high, along a narrow curve on the stage that circumnavigated a platform that, hidden by a velvet curtain, plummeted several stories into the basement as I walked by. The eyes never gaze down unless the choreographer so requires.

For years, I took my feet for granted and cared for them as a dancer does: clipping the nails way too short and in curves that followed the joining of the nail to the nail bed; squeezing the lightly taped digits into punishingly tight dancer's shoes; routinely wearing obscenely high heels when away from rehearsal halls to recapture in public the command of the stage.

When sudden pain in my right foot crippled my pedestrian escapades several years ago, I sought podiatric advice for dealing with the problem. I soon learned that diagnosis ended when I mentioned that I danced when I was young: Doctors simply stopped looking once they knew my history. Custom shoe inserts solved one ache but exacerbated another; a program of massage and stretching relieved some pains, but did nothing for the arthritis creeping into my ankles and toes.

The story is the same and worse for polio survivors like my father. "Our physicians do not listen to us," one polio support group Web site observes.[*] Because it was nearly eradicated in this country with the introduction of vaccines in the 1950s, few doctors practicing medicine today have any experience with the disease. Yet some 300,000 of the estimated 1.6 million survivors of polio in the US are at risk for post-polio syndrome, a return of symptoms such as joint pain, muscle weakness, and even atrophy in the tissues that were afflicted so many years before. Endless fatigue and depression are also common complaints.

---

[*]   Barbara Goldstein, "The Late Effects of Polio: Post-Polio Syndrome," Florida East Coast Post-Polio Group, http://home.iag.net/~bgold.

As I unwound the tape with which I'd wrapped my toes to counter the blisters that surfaced when the clunky, unfashionable shoes I'd adopted for daily wear failed me on the first day at the golf tournament, I muttered with chagrin that I'd walked all over my feet and never even said I was sorry. I'd even bought a new pair of high heels recently—interview shoes—because try as I might, I cannot adjust to the look of a suit with clodhoppers and need that extra few inches for confidence.

"Be careful where you let your dogs run," the trapper cautioned us, and then he took us on a tour of the area, pointing out the hidden, gaping traps, set to snap cruelly onto a victim's leg should a poor creature wander too near.

We'd always found the desert filled with natural and manmade surprises, from the profusion of wildflowers that appear after a summer rain to a dam built in a dry arroyo far from the city and any hint of flowing water, marked WPA—the Works Progress Administration, part of the New Deal programs Roosevelt devised to put Americans to work during the Great Depression. But nothing surprised us more than meeting this trapper who was returning to civilization to sell his furs after who knows how long spent in the wild.

I arrived here, in this role, in this spot, the same way a tumbleweed finds a barbed wire fence. I am an accidental academic: I was rootless once I gave up dance, and drifted in on a prevailing wind. It was on one of our walks that we discussed what I might do if I left my staff position at the university. I returned to graduate school and chose my subject because it seemed to fit my aptitudes and I could study in the town where we lived. I earned my degrees in order to earn a living. We left the southwest and ended up in a new community chosen because it offered convenient proximity to my husband's family and his new job. And one day with sudden surprise, I realized that here in the city, we lived only a short distance from where the trapper said he'd gotten his start as a child, catching squirrels and other small animals and sending the skins in to Sears Roebuck as currency to exchange for goods.

Long after I quit dancing, I kept my character shoes, a kind of old-fashioned, moderately heeled shoe used for traditional dances or tap dance when small metal plates have been nailed to the toes and heels. I wore them, or other high heels, whenever I wanted to recapture that sense of command on the stage.

> Today into my dancing shoes my aging feet will clamber
> And though my feet forget the tune, the shoes, my shoes, remember.
>
> So while my steps are now routine and regular in their rhythm
> My shoes remember melodies, toes tingling within them
>
> And for today I'll dance again though I don't care to show it
> My heart will sing that secret song and no one else shall know it.

7

BUTTOCKS

While I am grateful to Jennifer Lopez for popularizing the ample posterior, I am simply not ready to accept the butt brassiere. In my youth, *lift and separate* referred to a desirable effect upon the breasts rather than the buttocks, and so I was more than a little surprised at the rear view image in the three-way dressing room mirror that greeted me after I squeezed into the elastic girdle proffered by the salesgirl at Victoria's Secret. Clearly, the she mistook my purpose: my goal was to *restrain* my protuberant behind, not to plump it up like a pair of goosedown pillows.

My hunt for the proper foundation garments was inspired by my need to find just the right balance between corporate attire and theatrical costume suitable for a conference talk I would be giving on the tango and tacit knowledge in technical texts. Over the years, I'd learned it was essential for me to adopt the right costume for scholarly debates. Although words are the currency of academic exchange, the body is the vessel that forms them. I expected conference attendees, many of them men, would be skeptical about the connections I saw between dancing the tango and developing texts such as engineering drawings or patent documents. I wanted my appearance at the conference to reflect the tension and excitement of the comparison I would be drawing. To my amazement, I'd found just the right outfit: a long-sleeved, two-piece dress that evoked *tango* in its red-and-black color scheme and lightly ruffled neck, sleeves and hem, yet suggested *suit* by the basic cut and closure of the top and the modest neck- and hemlines. The dress was perfect.

I, however, was not, and the close-fitting, slightly sheer garment revealed my imperfections. In my youth, experience taught me that even at a fit and firm 118 pounds, my *gluteus* was sufficiently *maximus* to inspire the occasional condescending comment. "Yer butt's too big" an inebriated oaf slurred once when I was out with college friends at a bar. "Your mouth's too big," I wanted to reply but did not, as at seventeen my own mouth was still corseted with courtesy. That term's ballet teacher, a prepubescent nymph from New York City, trilled the same tune: "You've got a cute figure, dear, but it's just not right for dance." My butt condemned my budding career in ballet.

Once I hit forty, I observed with some dismay that my formerly taut physique suddenly turned to silly putty. Thwacking one hip was like tossing a pebble in a pond: I could watch ripples reverberate from one side to the other. In fact, there was no need for thwacking to create imperfections in the surface of my formerly smooth thighs, newly dimpled by cellulite. And despite months of exercise, movement still incited a certain jelly-like jiggling, so modesty decreed I seek artificial means of control.

According to Zona, an Internet Web site devoted to girdle history and lore, the girdle has been smoothing women's posterior regions for nearly one hundred years.[*] Zona explains that their popularity waned during the sixties' sexual revolution with the introduction of mini-skirts, beneath which a girdle might immodestly peek. It seems to me, however, that if women were setting their bosoms free, they might as well release the restraints on their nether regions. I suspect we lack tales of girdle-burning, however, because unlike the brassiere, the girdle cannot be removed with a mere flick of the fingers, a spontaneous act suitable to mob enthusiasm. Just try to imagine groups of women gathered 'round a bonfire bent over in a tug-of-war to free themselves from the grip of these elastic undergar-

---

[*] Virginian, "The Girdle Encyclopedia," Zona: The Girdle Zone, http://www.girdlezone.org/encyc01.htm

ments. The thrill would pass long before the fires were first stoked with the offending undergear.

Which brings me back to my search for the appropriate undergarments for my tango suit. Zona identifies four types of modern girdles: the *panty girdle*; the *open-bottom girdle* and its sister, the *hip-slip*; the *control brief*; and the *all-in-one*, which mercilessly combines brassiere and girdle into a single undergarment that constrains the figure *and* the ability to exercise certain bodily functions within a reasonable amount of time. I'd imagined that the perfect solution for my dilemma would be a hybrid of the hip-slip and the all-in-one: a bra/slip contraption that would provide appropriate support both above and below the waist, yet make allowances for the nervous peeing I often experience before speaking. I never realized until I tried to get into one of these garments the misfortune of my habitual method for putting on a brassiere. Perhaps only women with very large breasts develop the manual dexterity necessary to fasten a brassiere in back; after at least ten minutes of sometimes violent struggle in the dressing room, I can personally attest to the physical impossibility of fastening the rear clasp of the brassiere portion of the bra/slip at the front of my body and then wrenching the entire garment around to its proper conformation, with the padded breast cups actually facing forward.

In the end, I opted for a multi-piece solution to my undergarment needs: camisole and half-slip, plus padded bra and panty girdle of the traditional type, one more akin to those my mother wore than that of such apparent appeal today. I suppose I should have been prepared to experience a generation gap in lingerie; I certainly had not imagined even my undergarments could show my age. But only a woman without hemorrhoids wears thong underwear, and I'll leave the Wonderbutt to the young.

I liked the image the mirror reflected: I smiled secretly as I admired the appearance of slender curves and smooth muscles the long-sleeved unitard and the body within it created. I'd searched specifically for this type of garment to wear to the exercise class my husband and I attended. I'd purchased it to celebrate the re-awakening of my physical self and the return to a disciplined exercise regime after years of benign neglect.

As a dancer, you develop mercurial relationships with the mirror, the scale, and the image of your body both impart. The mirror is a teacher who helps you see when your movements soar and when they falter. She helps you learn the essence of artistry so that when she is replaced by the proscenium arch, you know the power in performance and you can fly. Her partner, the scale, is a merciless critic who reminds you that food is the enemy with whom you do battle throughout each day. "A moment on the lips, a lifetime on the hips," he groans. "Eat it today, sit on it tomorrow." Together, the mirror and the scale engender the obsessive unselfconsciousness needed to dance with abandon and the vain self-repugnance needed to improve.

Those behaviors now recognized as eating disorders were not problems but solutions for myself and for my friends. "I've finally figured it out!" cheered a girlfriend as she clambered out of her street clothes and into a leotard and tights. "I know how I can make my weight requirement and still have dinner out with my boyfriend!" Unlike the television images of anorexic and bulimic girls tortured by self-loathing, we spoke openly and dispassionately among ourselves about the strategies we used to manage our weight.

The irony of the weight requirement—and the weekly public weigh-ins that were part of life in the ballet program at the university—was that the pressure created in me a problem that had never existed before. I entered the program slender in comparison to the general population on campus, yet discovered for the first time I was "over weight." In vain attempts to gain control over my firmly muscled girth, I began experiments with fad diets, purging after meals with and without the aid of ipecac, and ultimately, in Vegas, with tiny little pills the girlfriend who'd given them to me called *white cross*.

These diet pills were methamphetamines, a form of speed. They were presumably safe to use under the supervision of a physician, but certainly suspect under the conditions by which I'd obtained them. And according to information from the National Institute on Drug Abuse, the stimulant can cause permanent and devastating damage to the central nervous system.[*] Ironically, this drug that might make me thin enough to dance (according to my critics) could compromise my very ability to do so by causing symptoms similar to those of Parkinson's disease including tremors, stiffness, slowness, and impaired balance.

In one way, I knew first hand of the risk I faced. Years before, the choking anguish in my father's voice when he woke my mother and told her that the police had come late that night looking for my brother had been enough to inoculate me from the temptations of alcohol, pot, and other drugs. That event got my attention; it got my brother's, too. Although we'd always had a troubled relationship, this was one subject upon which I trusted his judgment and advice above all others.

"When I got your letter," he wrote, "I just dropped everything to write you this one. Don't mess with speed. It is real easy to become addicted to."

I grinned at his next words—"It is also real bad for your health"—then grimaced at the alternative he suggested. There would be no quick fixes in a regimen that included natural vitamins, whole foods, and energy shakes made with nutritional yeast, lecithin, yogurt, and fresh fruit.

I'd like to be able to say that flushing the drugs down the toilet and buying a blender with my first real paycheck marked a change in my relationship with my body, but that would only come years later after I entered counseling and grieved the loss of my sister and my career. I

---

[*]   National Institute on Drug Abuse, "NIDA InfoFacts: Methamphetamine," http://www.nida.nih.gov/Infofax/methamphetamine.html

learned to cover the mirror, ignore the scale, and begin to love myself as I am.

These old foes were recently roused by the renewed attention to my body stimulated by the success of the change in diet my husband and I had begun the year before. We both had plenty of clothes in our closets that we could no longer wear, and welcomed the possibility of regaining our wardrobes by losing some weight. The plan we followed was a sound one, endorsed by a wide variety of experts.

To my surprise, our friends applauded my husband's forty-pound weight loss yet remarked with concern at my ten. At 120 or so pounds, I was still well above my ideal dancing weight and within normal ranges for my body type and height. But even my physician was less than impressed. "Do *not* lose any more weight," he commanded. I grew defensive about the diet when talking to others, explaining that my goal was not to lose weight but rather to rid myself of sugar addiction given the high incidence of Type 2 diabetes in my family. I felt conflicted each time I stepped on the scale. Hadn't I exorcised these old demons? Was there really something twisted and dark within me that drove me toward self-starvation? Wasn't it ok to feel satisfied that I could fit once again into clothes I'd worn just a few years ago?

The act of losing weight is fraught with issues of identity, and today I recognize that in the struggle to control my size I donned an internal corset from which I have yet to be loosed. While I take secret pleasure in my reflection, I know the image in the mirror is an illusion: no matter how long and hard I look into the glass, I still cannot see what is real.

I congratulated myself on my good fortune as I looked around the crowded waiting room. Apparently, the doctor was more than just a well-regarded specialist—a hand surgeon of great skill—but, judging from the sea of bandaged appendages that surrounded me, he was a *left*-hand surgery specialist. The woman who struggled to free her heavily bandaged hand from the elasticized cuff of her bulky winter coat; the middle-aged workman with band-aids on his fingers and gauze wrapping hand and wrist; the elderly woman who sat across from me, her hand and arm sheathed in a neoprene glove—all nursed gauche wounds.

I was there because I believed that I had broken a bone in my left hand the previous January when, in one of those classic struggles suited for a survivors show on reality television, I sought to do the near impossible: to stand up gracefully from my seated position in a rocking recliner. I began by placing two hands on the armrests, and as I pushed myself upward, felt the SNAP! in my left hand and swore with the unexpected pain as I fell back into the seat.

I was sure I'd broken a bone. The pain was the same as I had felt the first time I had broken a bone as an adult, also in a similarly death-defying feat. That time, I had fractured one of my metatarsals when I opened the screen door and stepped out onto the back porch. The slightly awkward and off-balance weight transfer was enough to send me driving left-footed to the nearby prompt-care center. I hopped through the doorway, signed in, declared what ailed me and took a seat as directed, only to be asked after I'd settled to return to the counter across the room where the receptionist had plopped down a clipboard filled with the obligatory paperwork. "I'm here because I *think* I *broke* my *foot*," I remarked as politely as I could, given the pain in my foot and the surprising request. "Is there any way you could possibly bring the clipboard to me?"

That time, the fracture showed up on the x-rays and I left the facility on crutches sporting a neon-green, knee-high cast and gained my first real lessons in the need for better handicapped parking and access to buildings on campus. Access routes must have been designed by a team made up of several undergraduate psychology majors, an inebriated architect, and a traffic engineer with a twisted sense of humor. I could park directly in front of the round, two-story building where I worked and walk up a long, winding ramp to get to the second floor, but because the building had no elevator, to reach my office on the first floor I had to open a series of heavy doors and descend several flights of steep stairs on crutches. If I wanted to avoid the stairs, I had to hobble up the street past several large buildings to the corner, turn and follow a sidewalk that gradually sloped downhill, then backtrack the length of a city block to access the first floor at the rear of the building.

This time, no fracture could be seen on the initial x-rays of my hand and wrist, so I was sent home with instructions to use ice and analgesics. Results from the DEXA-scan the doctor ordered were less encouraging. A DEXA-scan measures bone density, and already my bones were thinner than they should have been.

"You could be the poster child for osteoporosis," my family physician had remarked, "except that you don't smoke." What he meant is that I have a good number of the risk factors for the pernicious ailment, a disease that affects more than half of women over the age of fifty that can result in debilitating injuries and can severely compromise quality of life or even lead to death. Some of the risk factors are hereditary: I am female, white, slight, and have a family history of osteoporosis. Others have to do with how well I've cared for myself: I over-exercised and barely escaped chronic eating disorders in my teens and early twenties, starving my bones of nutrients essential to laying down layers of calcium during the years bone growth should have been most active. Though I enjoy walking on campus and downtown, I'm neither as fit nor as flexible as I once was. I've never been a big milk drinker and have never taken multivitamins or other supplements with any regularity. After menopause, when my body stops making estrogen, I'll be even more at risk because estrogen helps prevent bone loss.

So what does it mean for a woman in her mid-forties to be a poster child? Imagine a poster captioned "Not This!" illustrated with the image of a boney ballerina with graying hair wearing a Shirley Temple dress, pillbox hat, white tights, and patent leather Mary Janes looking up to shake hands with a burly politician. Definitely a frightening figure in these days of epidemic obesity, a model for public fear. How many actresses and models would be put out of work if in the minds of the public, their size became linked with debilitating disease? How many female dancers and athletes might be shunned for their sinewy, lean, and overly muscular builds? In this age when being *too fat* is bad and being *too thin* is bad, I think I'd rather be likened to Goldilocks, who finally finds what's *just right*.

The pain in my hand, though it seemed to go away after while, never completely disappeared. A summer of terrible golf (I couldn't grip the club and comfortably cock my wrist) plus mysterious episodes of sudden, severe pain sent me seeking a second opinion months later. This time, x-rays from clever angles showed a likely culprit: a *non-united fracture on the hook of the hamate*. Translation: I had floaty bone in my palm, a problem that could be corrected by surgery.

Unfortunately, though I had repeatedly had trouble with my left hand and wrist, no amount of prodding or poking by the surgeon could elicit pain. The same was true on the second visit as well as the third, even though I'd twice re-injured my hand in the intervening weeks, once by reaching in my pocket and another time by tucking in my shirt.

It may be that the surgeon I chose is considered the best in town because he's careful: if there's pathology but he observes no pain and there is no projected serious outcome, he recommends restraint. The doctor has suggested that, for now, I simply do the things I want to do and give him a call if the pain shows up again. It might be that if I actually started the weight-training program I'm supposed to do to build my bones, the pain in my hand and wrist would make its appearance on cue. For the time being, though, I guess I'll take my calcium, attend to my diet, and consider this my official entry into the age of aches and pains.

8

FACE

In that fleeting feminist moment, I assumed what I imagined to be a serious, dignified expression appropriate to a university professor. "Men aren't expected to smile for ID photos," my idle mind chatted, "so why should I?"

"Oh my," I thought, as I glanced at the camera's handiwork. Perhaps this was one of those moments when theory and practice should have parted ways. The ex-convict image that glowered at me from the small plastic card suggested I might have reconsidered my philosophy more carefully had I known of the outcome in advance.

What bothered me most about my winning entry in the worst faculty photo contest, though, was the unassailable confirmation that all the sun I had enjoyed the previous summer when I painted the trim on the house as we prepared it for sale had indeed left my face with a distinctive mustache-and-goatee "tan." I found this particularly disturbing as I had just that day abandoned my usual face *au naturale* and troweled on several layers of liquid foundation in preparation for the photo session, just in case the shadows I thought I saw on my upper lip and chin weren't the result of bad bathroom lighting.

This skin condition, called *melasma*, commonly occurs when a woman is pregnant or taking oral contraceptives. It can also be caused by naturally occurring hormonal imbalances. For me, it was the first undeniable sign that my forty-year-old body was entering the change, a sort of puberty-in-reverse complete with both physical and emotional upheaval. My personal advice to aspiring women professionals is that early on you arrange things so that the most important phases in your work life coincide neither with child-bearing and rearing—which have been thought to derail even the most promising of careers—nor with midlife and menopause, which are less often mentioned as impediments to professional success, but which come with enormously unsettling changes that are exacerbated by stress.

Conservative care for melasma was easy to follow in the fall and winter months: stay out of the sun and wait for the tea-colored stains to fade. Accepting the discoloration, though faint, was harder, especially as I was starting a new job and wanted to make a good impression on my new colleagues and students. I'd grown accustomed to leaving my face bare aside from touching up the occasional peppering of acne (which has also revisited during these post-pubescent years), but I was mightily self-conscious about the paint-resistant, male-patterned shadows on my face.

Several decades years prior, I had adopted my pallid armor out of convenience and as a feminist statement of acceptance of my natural self and rejection of the artifice of the stage. Ironically, I'd also done so for cosmetic reasons: there's little point in applying mascara when your eyelids are adorned with but four individual lashes separated by large gaps, the intermittent result of an apparently untreatable stress-related condition that began during my brief stint in Las Vegas. Hyper-consciousness of my bald eyelids conveniently coincided with my need to abandon contact lenses and my feminist awakening in graduate school. I thought bald eyes would be less noticeable if I eschewed eye makeup altogether and adopted shaded eyewear instead. I rather thought it would be a side benefit if, as a result of my unpainted face, I was less often treated as a painted woman by men I neither knew nor cared to know.

I relished the separation of self from sexuality my bare face offered, although it was hard to give up on the idea of beauty. I only gave up on the rest of the items in my cosmetics bag—foundation, concealer, blush, lipstick—in my late twenties after I accidentally left the small bag of confidence at home and had to speak at a conference plain-faced. "The best cosmetic is a warm smile," I told myself after I'd made the dismal discovery. The talk went well enough and no one called for paramedics, and so I figured perhaps I'd carried it off.

Now I was once again faced, quite literally, with another reason to adjust my attitude toward my appearance. Eyebaldness plus the distinctively male-patterned melasma combined with emerging wrinkles and a sudden thicket of blonde hairs at the corners of my mouth convinced me that my smile no longer adequately compensated for changes wrought by time and shifting hormones. In my twenties, it was freeing to let go of beauty and embrace a certain plainness; in my forties, it was disturbing to have plainness defaced, my mirror now reflecting the bearded lady of carnival fame.

Folicular misbehavior was satisfactorily addressed by grip-it-and-rip-it home facial waxing. But what to do about the surface imperfections of my skin? I loathed the idea of using theatrical pancake makeup to paint my visage into fresco, knowing full well that even if I managed to avoid starting the day looking like a character from Madame Tussauds, altering my expression in the least, as I knew from experience, would wreak an earthquake of cracks in the plaster by day's end.

The answer to my facial woes came in five small pots of colored dust and a set of brushes for their subtle application. Guided by the infomercial's messianic mantra—swish, flick, brush, [repeat]—I buffed away discolorations and in less than five minutes, was miraculously left with a fresh, glowing, "natural" complexion.

I had no sooner solved the problem with my face than another problem arose. My crowning glory—long, thick tresses that had darkened in adulthood from a deep golden blonde to a warm medium brown—seemed overnight to have turned a particularly grim shade of dirty dishwater shot through with grimy floating white strings. I wasn't graying gracefully as my mother did, turning evenly from dark brunette to salt-and-pepper to silver gray. The truth was becoming increasingly clear: aging was an ugly problem I was going to have to solve. I could not be so certain that this perimenopausal morphing into a cartoon version of my former self would not affect my career. Philosophically, I believed a woman ought to be able to gray naturally. I admired a friend's glorious strawberries-in-snow and actually rather liked the concentrated streaks at my temples. But my perception was that youthful women have better chances of being hired—or getting tenure—than do gray-hairs. There's also that business about being asked if I was my sister's *mother*. The second time it happened, I decided I needed to shelve my principles and consider other alternatives, joining the millions of women who support the multi-billion dollar U.S. hair coloring industry.

My sister, whose career in opera demands a youthful demeanor, had been using home hair coloring products for several years with clearly beneficial results. The economy of this solution appealed to me, though by this time I had a record of committing myself to the act then hesitating interminably. Twice before, I'd purchased coloring kits, opened the boxes, read the directions, and left the kits in the bathroom cabinet under the sink while I gathered my nerve, a process that inevitably took so long I ended up digging through the dust and cobwebs to throw the products away because I was convinced the chemicals had decomposed like so much old paint in the garage. A bad dye job is just too public a humiliation to risk, and my fears inevitably called to mind a high school classmate who changed hair color about as often as most people change their sheets.

I concluded that finding a flattering shade might require significant experimentation. My sister's advice was to go into a beauty supply store and ask someone for assistance in selecting the right color. With the aid of a helpful clerk (the one who didn't sport the raspberry Mohawk), I ended up choosing a dark ash blonde instead of a warmer tone because I hoped to avoid the brassy red highlights that trumpeted "cheap blonde" when I'd streaked my hair in high school. I waited until the holiday break between semesters before opening the box, thinking that the flexibility of my schedule would at least allow me to don hats or headscarves until I could make it to the first available hairdresser if my mad experiment went terribly wrong.

"I remember the day I first figured out you can use chestnut to deal with brassy hair," I overheard one woman remark, "Everything they taught me in school was wrong."

"I can't believe people try to use ash to cover red—you're just fighting it," said the other, "You've got to work with it." The two women could not have been more different. The first was older, dainty and petite, wearing a tan ensemble of neatly pressed sleeveless shirt and shorts. Her hair was a rich, artificial shade of auburn and she had a slightly pinkish tinge to her freckled fair skin that grew deeper as the sun grew higher in the sky. She wore dark Hollywood sunglasses, a wide-brimmed straw hat, and melted waxy-red lipstick.

Her companion, a much younger woman, was a buxom linebacker with stubby red ponytails poking out beneath her baseball cap. She was heavily tattooed: barbed wire encircled her right ankle and upper arm, and a peacock spread its wings over her left calf from ankle to lower thigh in colors of red, orange, blue, yellow, green, and black.

I wished I'd heard their comments before I'd begun in earnest my experiments with home hair coloring kits. I should have known better than to embark upon such penny-wise/pound-foolish efforts. Mother, with all the best intentions, had long ago provided us with good reason to avoid home hair styling. There was the whack-and-giggle story Dad told about the first and only haircut she gave him after they were married. He reported afterward getting up very early the next day, putting on his hat and coat, and waiting outside the nearest barbershop until it opened, hoping that enough hair remained upon his pate that a barber might be able to straighten things out without shaving his head completely bald.

Then there was the time she trimmed my bangs. Things started out well enough—they really were too long, and just getting them short enough so I could see the world beneath them was no a small victory—but the slight cowlick at the hairline in the center of my forehead caused some unanticipated difficulty. Mother had often told me about how as a baby my hair had reminded her of the nursery rhyme:

> There was a little girl who had a little curl
> Right in the middle of her forehead

Like my bangs that day, things started out well enough as I struggled to sit perfectly still while she worked:

> And when she was good, she was very, very good

The problem lay in the last line of the poem:

> But when she was bad, she was horrid

With several impatient wiggles and a few fateful snips, my bangs grew progressively shorter ... and shorter ... and shorter, until I was left with toothbrush stubble at the top of my brow that *still* was crooked.

In the end, the home hair color was reasonably acceptable—there were no unexpected reds or greens or blues—but I could never carry out the process neatly. No matter how hard I tried, I simply could not confine the staining dyes to their proper location. Cover the counter and sink? The dye ends up on the floor. Cover the floor? The dye ends up on the walls. Cover the walls? Well ... I *still* cannot explain how the color ended up on the ceiling, but I suspect it has to do with untangling a knot in my hair and the resulting sudden flick of a dye-saturated comb. Given the hours I spent masking off the parts of myself and the parts of my home I wanted to protect from the dye, I doubt I saved any time compared to that required by a salon visit. I suspect also that the hundreds of dollars in cost-savings for salon visits that home hair care purveyors claim consumers will enjoy fail to account for the expense of repainting and reflooring one's bathroom every few months simply to conceal the stains from the unavoidable messy spills. "This," I thought to myself, "was *not* working." I determined it was time to seek professional help.

Since the hair on my head grows like a crop of thick and unruly weeds and I abhor visible roots on women who color their hair, I mulled over the costs and the consequences and decided that I should think of the salon treatments as a business expense, an investment in my personal financial future. Furthermore, this solution was much more palatable to my husband than the other alternative I proposed: shaving my head and wearing wigs.

I still swallow hard at the end of each visit to the hair salon when I pay the bill. I live with the small economy gained by keeping my hair cropped in a style that doesn't need a part, a strategy that allows me the harmless delusion that my roots don't show even if I wait five weeks between visits. Despite regular trips to the hair salon, I'm not convinced I really look younger than my years. Indeed, I have a small bit of empirical evidence to the contrary: "You *still* look good," a fellow on the street remarked one day in a lazy Southern drawl. "How old are you, forty-eight?" I laughed and shook my head as he overshot the mark by a good little bit (I could not help but wonder, what else is making me look old?) Perhaps in my next decade or so of life—assuming I survive the pressures at work—I'll embrace my inner crone and gladly don her silver coif.

9

TEETH and NAILS

Forget pomp and circumstance, high ideals, and talk of opening young minds. An academic job is a pissing contest in which participants claim ideas much like the wolves studied by Farley Mowat used urine to mark territorial boundaries.[*] My own introduction to "the strong feeling of property rights"[†] these wolves feel toward their work—however narrow its scope and minor its public impact—occurred in graduate school when I presented my first paper at an academic conference.

As a master's student, I had been encouraged by a professor to submit my modest inquiry into connections between Romantic literature and classical ballet to a conference sponsored by the Rocky Mountain Modern Language Association. I was genuinely surprised when it was accepted, and I naively believed that the goal of such conferences was to share ideas. I failed to observe the potential threat lurking among the four or five people who attended my session.

Even when you're trying to stake a claim, it can be difficult, as Mowat describes in his narrative. To get the attention of the wolves he studied, he used the wolves' technique and intentionally marked a path across their property by consuming large quantities of tea, and after letting nature take its course, depositing numerous yellow puddles near his tent.

Women are, quite naturally, disadvantaged in this area because even if we have the desire, we lack the hardware necessary to direct the strategic

---

[*]   Farley Mowat, *Never Cry Wolf,* (Boston: Little, Brown and Company, 1963).
[†]   Ibid., 82.

stream. Indeed, some women avoid altogether peeing away from home as they seem to share a near pathological fear of toilet seats, a self-perpetuating ailment as those who fear sitting are the same as those who make toilet seats fearful by their undisciplined showers of urine. (Request to readers who are guilty as charged: Lift the seat and *please* pee neatly.)

Yet women have had to adapt in order to scale the ivory tower and, as I was to learn, no wolf in nature is so vicious as the female academic threatened by even an unwitting interloper.

"Any questions?" I smiled widely as I opened the floor after reading the last line. I savored joyfulness in learning and sharing and thought to myself, "Aren't these a fun ideas to ponder?" as I awaited a first response.

A she-wolf in professional clothing issued a thinly veiled snarl, "What did you find from studying the musical scores of the ballets you describe?"

I hadn't studied the scores, the audience came to understand from my embarrassed response. I hadn't done so because in one crucial sense, I am illiterate. I might know a ballet intimately, every nuance of movement and note, but my kind of knowledge doesn't count among the lettered as like many dancers, I cannot read music. You don't learn a ballet from a score; you learn it from the choreographer, the music, the mirror, and the audience when you perform.

I'd peed on her rocks, she let me know with her damning questions, and she was ready and willing to fight over the intellectual territory she had claimed. Though I kept my composure during the session, her snapping teeth left deep marks.

My doctoral colloquium was the next public presentation I gave, and since my talk had *sexism* in the title—and since I had at least one particularly confrontational classmate who would be sure to attend—I felt it necessary to take protective measures.

First, I seeded the crowd, recruiting my female friends to come, listen, and share their strength. Then, I arrived early so I could practice for a few moments drawing my secret weapon from its hiding place beneath the lectern and replacing it when I was done.

People began to filter into the room. It was a good-sized crowd, most likely driven by curiosity, as I was among the first few students to make it this far through the relatively new doctoral program. My friends sat or stood throughout the room where I could clearly see their warm and supportive faces. I knew my pack was with me and I could draw upon their strength should a challenger wish to spar about my preliminary intellectual claims.

As I came to end of my talk, a large male in the middle of the crowd began to pace, circling and sniffing, hand ready to raise for the first question. But I was ready this time for attack. I made my last point, pulled out my weapon, bared my teeth in a wide and expansive smile, and asked, "Any questions?"

A ripple of gentle laughter spread through the crowd. I made eye contact with the large male, whose raised hand signaled readiness for battle. I grinned broadly as I responded to his challenge. Confused by my actions but unswayed from his original course, the large male pounced—and missed. He pounced again; I dodged. A few more parries and the large male withdrew, leaving me victorious having stood my ground at the front of the room. The construction hard hat I had pulled from the lectern and placed on my head had worked, simultaneously shielding me and disarming my challengers as I opened the floor for questions.

Despite this success, I continued to view conferences with caution. While I had once rather enjoyed the idea of the public speaking that my continuing education and my new profession would demand, I came to see conference presentations as competitions and I loathed the envy and the enmity they inspired.

Several years ago, I witnessed a repeat of my own first conference experience, except this time, the graduate student was speaking to a larger crowd and her tormentor, dressed in blood red and black, was a she-wolf clothed with the power of session moderator. She fawned over the words of the well-established scholars on the panel, and then to my surprise, the "moderator" sharpened her nails on the graduate student. Taking full advantage of her hold over the floor and advance reading of the papers, she sliced the student's argument into carefully carved ribbons, mindless of any effect but her own aggrandizement and oblivious to how disciplinary differences might influence research presented at this interdisciplinary conference on gender and science.

The wolf is in all women, according to author, analyst, and cantadora Clarissa Pinkola Estes, yet as she and Mowat discovered, the wolf is widely misunderstood. To Pinkola Estes, rage and the territoriality of wolves that Mowat observed (and to which I objected) are deeply intertwined. To grow, we must begin by giving voice to our own rage.

> It is a mistake for others to think that just because a woman is silent, it always means she approves of life as it is.
>
> There are times when it becomes imperative to release a rage that shakes the skies. There is a time ... to let loose all the firepower one has.[*]

Though rage may be righteous, it need not be destructive; as women, we might "make rage into a fire that cooks things rather than a fire of conflagration."[†]

After the session, my friends and I talked about the bloody baptism the graduate student had endured, an experience that might mark both her entry to and exit from the profession. Though she was a stranger to me and indeed a visitor to this country, I believed I knew where she

---

[*]   Clarissa Pinkola Estes, *Women Who Run With The Wolves: Myths and Stories of the Wild Woman Archetype*, (New York: Ballantine Books, 1992), 361.
[†]   Ibid., 364.

was—alone in her hotel room—and how she felt—humiliated and infinitely diminished. Worse, I worried that the actions of one hateful female
would discourage her from attending the remaining sessions and getting
the most out of what otherwise promised to be a stimulating gathering.
Acting on a hunch, I dialed the hotel operator and asked to be connected
to her room if indeed the young lady was registered in the conference
hotel.

I could tell from her voice when she answered the phone that she had
been crying. I told her who I was, that I'd been in her session and enjoyed
her talk, that I was enraged by the way she'd been treated by the moderator, and asked if she would like to join me and my friends for a drink in
the hotel bar and hang out with us for awhile. Yes, she said, she would.

10

BACK and BELLY

My future will soon hang on my skill as a writer of fiction: *The Happy Tale of My Life at the University*. The key requirement—and the key challenge of this task—is to write a compelling story absent conflict. There is room for truth neither in the dossier nor in the process that constitutes a tenure-track faculty member's annual review. Tenure is a courtship in which one party woos and the other evades, providing only the most tepid response to good works and scrupulously documenting all faults so as to preserve power and the legal option to refuse an offer of the brass ring, the chance to remain employed at the end of a five-year audition.

I had felt stifled by my employment contract with a Fortune 500 firm, which specified that even freelance writing on my own time required written permission from the legal department. So I had eagerly embraced the opportunity for a one-year contract at the school. The job promised a chance to try my hand at teaching, but more important, a schedule that suggested there would be long months of unfettered freedom to think and to write. That first semester, I felt as I had as a child when I survived near drowning: I gulped in freedom as the air I needed to survive after being submerged for far too long. And though those first months had their challenges—a grueling commute across time zones and five new preps—I felt as if at long last I had found a professional community and an intellectual home.

That feeling faded the next semester during the final round of interviews for a permanent position, the much coveted tenure-track job. Given

my congenial welcome and the accolades I'd received for my prior professional work, I was confident about my chances, especially when the appli-
cant I'd viewed as my most serious competition withdrew. But when the
department head called me to her office to ask if I really wanted my on-
campus "visit" to include all the usual events—a campus tour, breakfast
and dinner with faculty, and so forth—I saw my true standing. I would be
a cheap date, saving the department hiring budget a few dollars from the
typically bloated expenses of the faculty hiring circus. Though at the time
I'd considered her actions thoughtfully solicitous (and indeed, perhaps
that was the intent), I later realized that by curtailing these activities I lost
precious opportunities to interact with members of the department I had
not yet met.

The last to be interviewed, my abbreviated visit had hardly concluded
before my remaining competitor called to pressure the department for the
job. She had several other offers in hand, but this university was her first
choice. The department head buckled immediately. Unwilling to wait a
couple of days for the scheduled vote, she called an emergency meeting so
the faculty could decide to whom the offer would go and by that action
signaled her choice. I waited alone for news of the department's decision
in the two-room cottage I inhabited each week and gathered the outcome
from the stillness of the night.

The next morning I steeled myself for the day, hoping to maintain my
composure given the embarrassment of rejection. I arrived on campus
early, as was my habit. It would be several hours before the department
office would open and I hoped to finish making the photocopies I'd need
for class before meeting any of my colleagues. I slipped my key into the
lock, jiggling it impatiently to coax the worn tumblers. When finally the
stubborn lock relented, I closed the door instead of propping it open for
others so I could hear if someone else approached. I flipped the switch on
the ancient machine and waited for it to warm up.

My body stiffened when I heard a jingling of keys at the lock in the door behind me as the copier cranked out the last batch of handouts. Surprised at finding the room occupied, a colleague entered and blustered his condolences when he suddenly recognized me, clearly assuming that I had been informed of my fate. I composed a stiff smile—the best I could manage—and turned to tell him I had not yet had any official word, but I appreciated his gesture. I gathered my papers and retreated hurriedly to my office, once again closing the door behind me so that I might wait undisturbed and prepare for class.

My solitude was short-lived. Several others knocked on my office door and offered kind words and awkward explanations. One person volunteered that the hiring committee's vote was in my favor, but the department failed to support the recommendation of the committee. The discussion before the vote was heated, and the vote itself was close. The mask that was my face crumbled a bit with each new fragment of information. The tears that pricked behind my eyes became more insistent. My voice wavered as I tried to thank each one graciously and explain that still I was waiting to hear from the department head.

Hours later, and just five minutes before my first class, the department head confronted me as I was leaving my office to teach.

"I can't do this right now," I pleaded, "I have to go and teach my class."

She blocked the doorway with her body and granted me no quarter, speaking until she'd cleared her mind, stripping me of any shred of dignity before releasing me late to meet my students.

In the weeks that followed, the faculty member who had recruited me to the department tendered his resignation: he'd been offered a position as department head at another university. It may be that the faculty anticipated this departure and voted as they did because they knew I desired to stay in the area and they hoped to gain two new colleagues through a single hiring cycle. But doing so required the wheels of university bureaucracy to turn with unaccustomed speed as by convention, a year would typically be allowed to elapse in case the recently departed wished to return. Seeking to confirm my interest, the department head told me of the possibility for a position and several times asked for my response.

"Talk to me when you have a job to offer," I repeatedly replied. By the time I received the bittersweet offer from the university, I had two others to consider. Though ultimately I decided to stay, I've never been able to shake the sense of being the booby-prize hire, last choice in a pool of two.

The dossier is an exhaustive history of three kinds of contributions a faculty member is expected to make to the department, the university, and the community. Here, the writer constructs an argument for lasting acceptance into a community of scholars by describing her research, teaching, and scholarship. It is a part of the employee's permanent record and subject to scrutiny by others at every level of the academic hierarchy. The dossier and written feedback from evaluation committees have come to be central in legal arguments of competence and suitability as colleges and universities have been pressured to justify unfavorable decisions in what remains at essence a popularity contest.

I expected my publication record would not be an issue: I am a writer and I write. But teaching was identified early on as a weakness in my work. This was no surprise at first, given my years in corporate life and thus limited prior experience with semester-long courses. I'd planned to devote the greater part of my attention to developing my courses and my teaching skills during the first few years so that once I had some confidence in the classroom, I could refocus on research and writing.

That confidence never came. Having brought to the academy the team player perspective that had served me well in industry, I had without a second thought accepted the challenge and the learning opportunity of covering classes less directly suited to my education and experience when I was told other newcomers had requested those courses I'd found most interesting and exciting. I failed to recognize that thoughtfulness of others has no place in an academic career.

Then the content of the courses I was now scheduled to teach came under scrutiny. I had been somewhat stymied by several unsuccessful efforts to gain some background information about the curriculum and the courses that I had been assigned before I first taught them. Like most new teachers, I had hoped to learn their purpose, their fit in the program, and to get some ideas for suitable textbooks and assignments before teaching my first classes. Despite my efforts, I'd been given few details about what was expected, and so I drew upon my career experiences and my creativity to develop classes that would not only match my own strengths and stimulate student interest but include material and assignments that I believed would help to position our graduates favorably for their future careers. When several curriculum meetings were scheduled that fall, I looked forward to them with great excitement, hoping that at last I might gain a clearer sense of perspective and purpose. One of my courses was first up for review, and I was eager for feedback.

To my surprise, the meeting began with criticism: there was too much analysis, my colleagues stated, and not enough writing in the course I'd planned. The key culminating project—an electronic portfolio assignment that I'd crafted—wasn't appropriate for the class. My own assignment belonged not in my course, but in one taught by Sarah, the first-choice hire. I sat in stunned silence as my course was stripped of all I felt most excited about teaching and I was denied even a moment to explain the rationale behind the careful structure and sequence of assignments I'd developed. I felt tricked into exposing the softness of my belly, cut open and eviscerated, left with nothing—no ideas for texts, no suggestions for assignments for the next semester's work, and only a few weeks left before I'd have to select new textbooks for the course. That spring, the course was a disaster as I flailed about trying to find a focus and a purpose that would meet the vague requirements I'd been given and match anything I would be comfortable with in the classroom.

I'd said nothing in my defense during the curriculum meeting and grew wary of my colleagues, many of whom had been the most supportive during the hiring process. I quietly focused my attention on a different course that had as yet escaped their interest. Desiring to create an opportunity through which I might present my students with specific problems in communicating with clients, I developed what I described as an interactive case study: a set of facts and circumstances with a fictional client with whom my students would interact via electronic mail. I had an ally several states away who helped me assemble the materials for the case, such as photographs and factual background information. More important, I contrived behind the scenes to control email exchanges between the students and the "client," so I might at strategic moments confront students with the kinds of communication challenges that often must be managed in client projects.

I told my students the truth about the case: that parts of the project were real and parts were not, and that I had set things up so I would see all email exchanges between them and the client. I also told them that I wouldn't reveal what was fact and what was fiction because one key purpose of the assignment was to create a safe experience through which they could develop the client interaction skills they'd need for the final project of the semester when they'd be working with a real client on their own. Indeed, the critical element was that mix: I needed the students to believe in the details strongly enough to take the assignment seriously.

Gleeful about the idea for the interactive case, I'd shared its secret with only two colleagues. The assignment, and indeed the whole semester, worked exceedingly well, with the result that I was nominated for an Outstanding Teacher Award at the term's conclusion. But my relief at having at least one class well in hand was premature: quite by accident, I learned from one of my confidantes that someone—presumably the only other person I had told—had revealed the secrets of the project to the students, thus sabotaging my ability to repeat the interactive case with future classes. I said nothing about this malicious mischief as I did not want to rock the boat and started the work of re-creating over again yet another course.

I failed to recognize the consequences of my silence until it became clear that I'd have little opportunity during my probationary years to teach anything other than the courses I was now assigned. It gradually dawned on me that within our program, courses did not rotate; having given up my favorite classes to others when asked, I would not have the opportunity to teach them again in the foreseeable future. Having adopted courses I'd found challenging only to have them gutted of their most creative elements, I lost the motivation to innovate in the classroom and the bright spots in my teaching record faded with each new set of dismal student evaluations. I began to recognize the deleterious effects of my second-class citizenship within the department. I tested my suspicions by requesting a course I'd been asked to relinquish to my one-time competitor for the job when she joined the faculty.

My request was refused without hesitation: "We don't change courses during the probationary years."

And as my features hardened with a look of stony incredulity, a whispered explanation followed. "Sarah might not get tenure. She gets an extra year because she hasn't published."

Then came the offer to take away any course I wanted from an adjunct professor, one considerably more burdened than any of us and much lower upon the academic hierarchy. I refused the offer (perhaps foolishly, given the circumstances), but I would not do to another what had been done to me.

I had committed myself to welcoming Sarah with open arms when I decided to join the faculty, yet she had responded to my overtures with disinterest. Preoccupied by their own concerns, my senior colleagues did not notice the chasm that gaped between us. Cast as outsider, I withered and withdrew.

My dossier is silent on these facts, for the document is at once a record of individual accomplishment and a mirror of my experiences with those who are my judges. To reflect unfavorably upon circumstances to which my colleagues had been complicit would be to shine light in some dark and neglected corners. Flip a switch and the roaches scatter: when it mentions others, the dossier speaks of only what you might see in the most favorable light.

So the document overlooks the possibility that four students I caught one year in a nasty plagiarism case might speak unfavorably about me in student evaluations in required classes they took from me later. The document omits discussion of how during yet another semester, privacy laws demanded my own anguished silence in refusing information to a mother who telephoned one day, fearful her son might have hung himself in his dorm room and frantic to discover if he were dead or alive. The document is silent about the semester when a student in one of my classes threatened to kill the director and all the faculty members in our program. It says nothing of the tightrope I and my colleagues walked that semester trying to balance some semblance of authority with the need to keep from pushing him over the edge.

I was the one constant in the inconsistent numbers I received on student evaluations. No one ever asked me what I thought might help to improve my numbers. In fact, no one ever spoke to me about my evaluations at all, though on paper, I was criticized persistently about my record and required to participate in externally prescribed efforts to fix what my judges considered broken in my classrooms: Me.

11

BRAIN

Like other bits of needlework from my mother's family—doilies, cuffs and collars, and even a pair of fragile tatted gloves—the hand crocheted tablecloth was a fixture of my childhood, and I admired it as I explored the dainties stored in the china cabinet drawers. Another favorite among the treasures was a tiny sombrero, hand-crocheted in bright, multicolored thread, sized so a sewing thimble fit snugly in the crown of the hat, the tip of which, above the thimble, was stuffed with a bit of cotton so the hat would maintain an authentic shape. A small crocheted disk and a circle of gray felt had been attached with a few stitches at the brim of the hat, hinged to provide access to the sewing needles pinned to the felt inside. The tidy crocheted stitches, the use of variegated thread, and the whimsy of the project identified it as something that had been made by my grandmother's sister, my great aunt Olive.

Aunt Olive was a hundred years old by the time failing health and shocking frailty finally convinced her to let Mom pack most of her belongings for storage and bundle her and a few prized possessions off to Colorado Springs where my parents had retired. Aunt Olive had reached the point where she was no longer able to live independently and to remain healthy. She couldn't see well enough to recognize mold on cottage cheese in the refrigerator, and her antiquated taste buds weren't able to tell fresh from fouled food. Although clear-minded and remarkably untouched by the ravages of senility, she had trouble remembering when, or if, she'd taken medication for one ailment or another. She had trouble with lameness, and with a loneliness interrupted only by an old television, occasional phone calls from family, and Sunday church-going and card-playing when she could get someone to give her a ride.

It had taken many years of gentle persuasion before my mother was able to convince Aunt Olive to leave her home of eighty-some years. She had been in the house since she had it built in the 1920s with her share of the Oklahoma oil money from wells on the family farm. She'd lived there as landlord and tenant, sometimes inhabiting the tiny back room while renting out the front part of the house. She'd made the place a home for a husband, and then stayed firmly planted when she divorced, no longer able to bear participating in a sham marriage that, although founded on genuine fondness, could not "cure" her husband of his private homosexuality. During World War II, she'd tended my mother and her sister while my grandmother worked and my grandfather was a prisoner of the Japanese. She offered friends, cousins, and generations of the family's children the safety and security of her tiny bungalow. It was to Aunt Olive's home we fled one summer when Mom and Dad went through a particularly rough patch in their marriage.

I thought I understood Aunt Olive's attachment to her home, but I could not comprehend her steely resistance to letting my mother care for her in her twilight days. After all, her prized independence was most limited by her own aging body; if she were with Mother, she would have someone to care for her daily needs and company to ease her loneliness. In the end, Aunt Olive spent only three years with Mom and Dad before she died in their home, grateful for every kindness and cognizant of the burden of her presence. "Kathy," she would caution me when I visited, "Kathy, whatever you do, don't live too long."

After Aunt Olive died, Mother, her sister Bonnie, and I cleaned the house and worked our way through the boxes that had been hurriedly packed three years earlier. Though not as bad as some, my aunt suffered from the hoarding disorder that has afflicted so many of the members of my family.

Haste, and consideration for my great aunt's feelings, meant little had been discarded when she left her home to move in with Mom, so there was an enormous amount of material to be thrown away: worn, rotten, and moth-eaten clothing and linens; rodent-ravaged newspapers and clippings; dime-store figurines and cheap dishes; decade after decade of carefully trimmed and saved obituaries of friends, of family members, and of celebrities Aunt Olive had admired.

Among the refuse, we had found family treasure: boxes of cards and letters saved over her very long lifetime. As we came across them, we sorted them according to year, passing the time and the tedium as we cleaned by reading out loud letters that caught our attention because of the date, an unusual postmark, or sometimes, just because. Eight poignant letters sent between 1950 and 1957 held precious clues about why Aunt Olive was afraid to leave her home.

September 30, 1950

Dear Olive:—

This is humiliation to have to write you from this institute. I was brought here by Caroline and a man, whose name I do not know, and left penniless. They took my rings and beads and all the other possessions I had. I have written to her repeatedly for money and clothes but she does not respond to my letters.

The letters were from Annie Mathew, a family friend and childless spinster like my aunt who had lived with my aunt and her family from time to time. Annie wrote to Aunt Olive from the state mental hospital, where her niece Caroline had deposited her one day after a drive through the countryside.

> I need some money and in the box you have of mine, there is a crocheted table cover. I have tried to sell it for $25, but you see I have not been successful. There is about $9.50 worth of thread in it, and if you will give me the price of the thread I will let you have it. I would give it to you for past favors but you see I am sorely in need of money. I have not enough to buy stamps, hairpins or even a hairnet.
>
> If I can get up to the city, I think I can do something about my affairs. Surely there is someone who will help me out of this predicament. I could say much about Sue and Caroline but a letter is no place to say it. Anyway, the least said is the easiest mended.

I asked Mother if she knew anything about this woman who wrote in such desperation to Aunt Olive. Yes, she said. She remembered visiting Annie Mathew at the asylum, which was called in jest "the east campus" of the nearby university, no doubt because the buildings once housed the first women's college in the state before they were turned over for use by a private sanitarium company in the late nineteenth century.

Though deceived and uprooted, Annie's spirits were good: "I am swell," she reported, "and that is pretty good. I will be 78 years old this winter." Then she asked about the family. Had Olive's brother remarried? What of my grandmother and her children? "Sure hope you can buy my table cover," the letter closed.

Annie wrote again in late January, to thank Olive for a Christmas card and the money and hairnets she had sent. She then continued:

> Now the object of this letter is to tell you that I want to come back to the city, but they won't let me out because of not having a home. The Doctor, superintendent of this hospital, told me to give her the name of some friend so I am sending yours and Mrs. Hattie Tucker, and I hope you say a lot of nice things about me. Sue came down here soon after I came and told so many bad things. It has made it hard for me to live, it was such an awful thing. I can hardly think of a woman doing such an unfriendly thing.

She told a little bit about her environment at the hospital. She lived in the women's ward, which she characterized as "the last stop out of the institution" for women who were well enough to return to their homes and who had homes to go to. A later letter provided additional details: the ward housed seventy-three or seventy-four women who got along pretty well, all of whom ate in a dining room which fed some 1,200 individuals three times a day. The ward was clean, there was enough to eat, and the nurses were kind. There was a dance on Fridays, a movie Saturday evening, and church on Sunday morning. "This is a very pretty place," she wrote, "and wonderful for such as it is intended."

Two years passed before the next letter, and it (and those that followed) spoke of an empty sameness of days during the dull, unending weeks, months, and years Annie spent at the hospital. "The place is just as you saw it—no change, only occasionally some woman goes home and another one comes," she wrote several months after one of my aunt's visits. "Things go on here in kind of a monotone way." Annie stopped going to church, the Friday dances, and the Saturday movies as over time her hearing began to fail and walking became a chore.

I am so homesick I can hardly stand it. Caroline and Sue seldom write and I have not heard from them for a long time so I hope you will write to me.

Sometimes I find a city paper and always read the spots off it because it tells me a smattering of what is going on in the old home town. When you write, tell me everything that has happened since I came away.

In 1953, the sister-in-law who'd said such bad things about Annie when she was committed, died and was buried next to Annie's brother. "I was very sorry that Sue died," Annie mourned. "They did not let me know so I could not come to the funeral." She asked Aunt Olive to clip the obituary from the paper and send it to her.

The few possessions Annie had left in a box at Aunt Olive's house seemed to anchor her to the world outside the hospital: "Do you still have my 2 house dresses, 1 street dress, and the crocheted table cover," she wrote. She asked again a year later, "Have you got my dresses yet, and also my table cover?" and twice in 1954, "Have you got my dresses and my table cover? I would like to have my dresses if I could get them." She urged Aunt Olive to hold on to her clothes and the table cover as if knowing they were kept safely at a place that she once had called home helped her to believe that she would one day be able to collect them herself. "Don't let anybody have them as I will want them when I come to the city. I will not be here forever. *God will deliver me some day.*"

The last letter Aunt Olive received was addressed by someone else's hand. Annie had little to say and for once, did not ask about the dresses and the tablecloth. She enlisted Aunt Olive's help in contacting her niece Caroline, whose address she had lost. She wasn't well, she reported, and she asked for news about Aunt Olive's family. "I suppose you are having some cloudy weather. We are here. Please write soon. Much love, Annie."

Judging from her letters, which were clear and lucid from first to last, the quiet secret of Annie Mathew's existence was that she wasn't crazy; she was committed to a madhouse by relatives because she was old, poor, and alone, a fate my Aunt Olive doubtless feared. During Annie Mathew's years at the mental hospital, electroconvulsive therapy (shock treatment) was widely used to treat and control severely disturbed patients in large institutional settings like the one where Annie lived. The treatment came to be considered abusive and sparked changes at mental hospitals across the country in the 1950s and '60s. "There has been or maybe there is now an investigation being made of this place," Annie wrote in one of her letters, "I don't know if what they found was either good or bad."

The quiet secret of our own family was that Mom had been hospitalized and had electroconvulsive therapy to treat the post partum depression that plagued her after Amy was born. The confusion and memory problems she suffered thereafter she always attributed to her treatment, although I expect some part of her symptoms were caused by the bipolar disorder with which she had also been diagnosed. Years later, when my brother wrestled with his emotions as his self-esteem plummeted and doctors urged treatment—while I was in college, before the MGM—I had to get a job so I could support more of my expenses as my parents chose a costly residential program over the standard medical treatment available locally to ensure my brother would not be subjected to the same brutal "cure."

Some would have considered the old cloth not worth the time it took for even a hasty repair. Its ecru threads still showed evidence of a few stains from use and revealed in the slight changes in color from one area of the cloth to another that its maker did not buy all the thread from the same dye lot. This was not the kind of meticulous work that Mother always did, and even though she had taught me how to crochet and I'd stitched a goodly amount of lace, there was no way I would be able to equal the kind of repair Mom would have done had she approached the task. Mother would have taken the time to match the color and weight of the threads and then re-woven the stitches so the repair was undetectable from the original. I pulled out needle and thread and did my best to mend the broken stitches in the old lace tablecloth that she had given me.

"Of all the things I've lost, I miss my mind the most," reads the text on a bookmark I once bought. Until the forgetfulness began (a natural part of aging, I'm told), I was more than half amused by the message. Now, when my mind suddenly blanks and I grope for names, or words, or meaning, I worry some.

12

HEART

On December 9, 2005, my mother mailed birthday cards on behalf of a rag doll to family and friends instead of the usual Christmas missive. It wasn't *really* a birthday card, the writer explained, but rather an invitation to play a special game during the coming weeks, through Christmas Day. Tucked inside one of the six, hand-cut and carefully folded packets enclosed with the birthday card was a small note marked with smiley and frowney faces that explained the identity of the sender:

You may have guessed by now that I am really a rag doll. That does not make me any less real! I don't know if I'm a Wednesday's child or not, but I certainly came into a world full of woe. My mommie made me as a project to help mend her own grieving heart while trying to make a special gift for my sister Lizzie.

I was conceived on another sister's birthday, December 9, 1970, and born some time between then and Christmas Day.

The sender of the letter was Raggedy Anna—the life-sized doll my mother made the year that Amy died—and Raggedy Anna wrote to ask recipients to make her glad by celebrating her birthday and playing the Glad game, which Mother had devised after seeing "PollyAnna" on *Masterpiece Theatre*. "Who was Amy?" the outside of another small packet inquired. "She was a beam of sunshine seemingly unaffected by the chaos of those terrible days when Mommie was so sick …"

I have not valued my mother's gifts. Her two afflictions—bipolar disorder plus partial (and now significant) deafness have often resulted in bizarre behaviors and curiously disconnected conversations that, more often than not, were a source of laughter in our home. We selectively omitted any mention of the darker moments in public conversation and often made sport of Mother's idiosyncracies. "Mom doesn't try to be funny," I once wrote for a Toastmaster's speech, "she just *is*." My humorous speech continued:

Mom used to be one of those people who sneeze implosively. You know, one of those people who gets all ready to sneeze and all that comes out is a tiny little "hcchhh," at best only half a sneeze. The doctor advised Mother to alter her sneezing habits, as half-sneezing was not good for her ears and could worsen the existing damage to her eardrums. One day, after she'd been doing pretty well with whole sneezes, she got a tickle in her nose and after a great build-up, cut loose with a tiny "hcchh."

"Bless," I responded.

"Thank," she replied, and we both collapsed in giggles.

I had always considered Mother's hearing problems to be the main source of the comical lapses in communication that were so common in our home. Sometimes, though, there was the suggestion that something else might be going on.

Eventually, the doctor advised Mom to have surgery to improve her hearing. After the surgery, she had to wear cotton in her ears for a while. This cotton had to be changed regularly, and Mom could practically do it in her sleep. I'll never forget: we were in the car going somewhere when the clock struck cotton-changing time. So, without batting an eye, my mother, while driving the car, deftly removed the cotton from her ears, and selected and shaped new bits of cotton, and then—I noted with some alarm—she began to put the cotton in her mouth.

I shouted, "Mom, what are you doing?" She looked at me, then at the cotton, smiled sheepishly and laughed, "I guess that's the wrong hole."

There was also the time she misplaced her hearing aids.

One Sunday morning at an early breakfast, Mom, quite nonchalantly, mentioned that she hadn't been able to find her hearing aids, and would we help her look for them? Fearing the worst (that my dog had chewed up yet another pair) we spent several hours searching in vain for Mom's aids. We finally gave up the search at Mom's request. She felt sure, she said, that they would turn up.

Towards midmorning, right before leaving for church, I said something to Mom. To my surprise, she reached to her ears and turned up the volume on her aids. "Mom," I cried, "where'd you find your hearing aids?" She stopped, and with her hands still at her ears, she laughed, "I guess they were in my ears all the time—I suppose that's why I wasn't worried!"

Her natural ability to laugh at her foibles masked a more profound truth: Mother is a woman of prodigious talents and exceptional sensitivity. The image on the front of the birthday-Christmas cards she sent that year illustrates this point. It was an intricate design of butterflies and blossoms whose wings spread and petals bloomed because of the ingenious ways she had cut and arranged the brightly colored fabrics. The photo on the back of the card—of the reverse side of the quilt—revealed the ornate stitching that completed "A Celebration of Life."

A few weeks after I had received the birthday-Christmas card, my sister called me from Colorado, where she was visiting our parents during the holidays. She was frantic with concern for Mother, yet when she explained what was going on—Mom was very happy, they were having lots of fun, Mom was unconcerned about logistical details for Christmas celebrations—I didn't understand what could possibly be wrong. How could joyfulness, especially during the holidays, be cause for concern? I called Mom to talk and heard only happiness in her voice.

Yet my sister and brother still insisted there was something terribly wrong, so I began to call frequently, daily, to talk to Mom or Dad or my siblings to see if I could glean some inkling of what worried them so. I certainly thought it was odd, though charmingly sentimental, that my mother's Christmas gift to my sister was a bag of fabric scraps, each of which had a story connected to one of Mother's fabulous quilts. But as I listened more closely, I also began to hear a stranger in Mother's voice, a stranger whose concerns I did not understand. After each call, I contacted one of my siblings to see if I could parse Mother's ramblings into what was real and what was real only to Mother.

She analyzed why voice mails she *knew* she had deleted suddenly reappeared: "the government is trying to see who they can trust and who they can't trust." She spoke in hushed tones about the highly placed Republican congressman who lived just blocks away and of the subtle signs she noticed that signaled secret visits from the President. Her everyday conversation became strewn with foreign and archaic terms, *thee's* and *thou's*, and phrases from French and Spanish, the languages she had studied in high school and college. And when she had no words for what she wanted to say, she replaced language with a rhythmic babble she seemed to think we could all understand. I heard in Mother's voice her gradual descent from joyfulness to paranoia, and, after the doctor put her back on the lithium from which she had been freed for a good number of years, her tumble into a well of despair so deep I feared she might never see sunlight again.

The secret to long-term friendships, I had discovered, was to be grateful for every moment of happy camaraderie and to expect nothing more: to allow my friends the space to be themselves, to have shifting priorities as time passed and as our lives changed, and still to welcome each shared moment as a gift. I was not so generous with my family, as my humorous speech relayed.

Though Mom doesn't hear as well as she might, she talks better (or maybe just more) than most, especially if there is a lot of news to catch up on. Now that we live in different cities and see each other seldom, visits are crowded with conversation.

As I had grown older and spent less time with Mother, I had become impatient with her antics and longed for more ordinary conversation.

I've noticed, though, that she doesn't seem to hear me when I say it's time for me to leave. So, boldly, I interject, "That's interesting, Mom." ... "I've got about five more minutes, ok?" ... "Three minutes, Mom" ... "Gotta go, Mom. Love you—bye!"

Worn by years of broken promises and unspoken hurts (the marks of my familial bonds), I received the quilt Mother presented to me after I finished my Ph.D. with ingratitude, holding her accountable for having failed to complete it by Christmas when she had gleefully announced the previous fall that I should expect a big surprise. "Thank you," I said coldly. In an effort to warm my chilly embrace, she showed me with childlike delight the ways she had tailored the quilt to honor my accomplishment, decorating the backing with mementos of my graduation: fabric transfers of the notice in the paper, warm wishes from friends, and her own special blessings. "May Truth, Love, and Beauty be your Guides as you step ... into the wide world of Wisdom," and on the label itself, "Made for Katherine Durack with much love from her mother."

"It's nice, Mom, I'm glad to have it," I said. "But giving it to me now doesn't make up for not getting it done by Christmas. You don't get 'credit' for promises you make and then break. I'd rather be truly surprised by a gift than disappointed yet again."

Mother quietly heeded my hateful words, and surprised me a few years later with a small, quilted wall-hanging. It was a whimsical gift, reminiscent of the brightly colored "Three Operatic Pigs" quilt she had made for my sister. Like the quilt she'd made for Lizzie, the purple cow in my quilt had both storybook and real life references: Gelett Burgess's poem, "I Never Saw a Purple Cow," and the ceramic purple cow I'd once treasured that Mother had swept from my dresser and smashed to the floor during *the chaos of those days when Mommie was so sick.* The quilt wasn't quite done, she said, but she wanted to ask my opinion about the final piece. She had made a companion for the quilt, a richly embellished heart embroidered with the words, *For love and for forgiveness ~ Mom.* "Where should I put it?" she asked.

It wasn't until years later—until I began this book—that I fully comprehended Mother's grief, and her strength. Amy was born in December, and I knew that each Christmas after her death was a painful reminder of loss because I felt that loss myself. What I had forgotten—or perhaps, never even realized—was that Amy's death in June 1970 happened just two days after my mother's birthday. Every six months for over thirty-five years—at Christmas and on her birthday—the calendar has reminded my mother of one critical moment, one hesitation, one tiny delay. When my brother came to tell her he'd discovered a charge on the bare wire connected to an electronic contraption he'd been working on in his room, Mother waited, choosing instead to finish folding the laundry with me, so I'd be ready to pack my clothes and go to Girl Scout camp. Attending to the needs of one daughter cost her the life of another. Could this be why, so often since then, she could not hear me speak?

Puzzling through the *why's?* and *why now's?* of Mother's dramatic decline, my siblings and I returned to the birthday-Christmas card for clues. We concluded the answer lay in one of the folded papers inside the packet labeled "Why share this story now?" On November 30, nine days before the anniversary of my dead sister's birth, Mother was confronted once again with loss. Both my father and my brother had been having heart pain and were in the hospital for stress tests. While Dad was ok, Mike's initial results were anomalous, suspicious. At this news, Mother's heart simply broke.

It later turned out that Mike's heart is strong and healthy. And Mom is "back" now, too—still goofy, still wonderfully creative, still warm, still strong, and still annoying at times. But what I now know is this: My mother might live for many, many years, but if ever the pain gets bad enough again, she could leave in a heartbeat.

13

THROAT

Determining to speak is not enough. Nor is it enough to shout alone in a closet or utter inaudibly in a crowd. Both instrument and ideas must be tuned. It was only after my voice became worn and ragged that I realized how deeply ingrained were my habits of silence.

Quite frankly, I should have figured out much sooner that I was the enemy as much as anyone I'd ever known. Who else could I blame for the non-infectious laryngitis that kept me from singing my first solo in high school chorus? For the bout of laryngitis that silenced me in Vegas? For my declining vocal power and endurance in the classroom? Why, when frightened, did I become completely mute?

The answer is this: Over a lifetime, my body developed habits for silencing my voice. I suspect I learned these habits in infancy, as many times my mother told me of how much I cried and how, in pain or anger or frustration, I would hold my breath until my tiny body began to turn blue. Worn by the relentless cacophony and terrified by my aching rage, she did the only thing she could to make me breathe again: she ignored me.

In the end, I learned habits of speech that matched my mother's behavior and my father's words ("Children are to be seen and not heard"). When speaking to close friends and loved ones, I unconsciously adopted a child's small voice. When speaking to others, I closed my throat and constricted the sound. After teaching for several years, I began to lose my voice halfway through class and could speak only with discomfort the rest of the time. Ultimately, the clinical result was *a mild to moderate dysphonia characterized by a raspy, back-focused hoarseness.*

An ear, nose, and throat specialist had ruled out any serious physiological cause and sent me to a vocal therapist, who videotaped my vocal cords in action, a process that requires the patient to emit a variety of impossible sounds and simultaneously avoid gagging while a therapist pulls your gauze-wrapped tongue to your navel and extends a videocamera-on-a-stick down your throat. From this exercise, I got the thrill of seeing my vocal cords on TV, learned that they were *out of phase,* and discovered that I was flabby in places I didn't even know I had muscles. In fact, there are thirteen muscles that control the vocal mechanism nestled in the larynx, and mine were in serious need of calisthenics.

At my voice therapist's urging, I adopted the motto, "Speak wet, pee pale." He recommended consuming vast quantities of water to keep my whistle wet, virtually ensuring that I would spend nearly as much time in the ladies room as in the classroom. And, he prescribed a series of exercises, which, he assured me, would help me relearn how to speak in a relaxed and natural voice with greater or lesser volume when appropriate (as long as I could keep from laughing out loud as I made the ridiculous sounds and spoke the nonsense he had prescribed).

I imagine there's some risk of being diagnosed with a mental condition while one is undergoing vocal therapy. After all, in one well-known study of psychiatry in the US, several researchers, having said only that they heard voices repeating "empty," "hollow," and "thud," were diagnosed with schizophrenia and admitted to twelve different American mental hospitals. Although the study indicates the researchers behaved normally thereafter, they were held for nearly three weeks on average and upon discharge, described as schizophrenics "in remission!"[*]

---

[*]   Referenced in Suzette Haden Elgin, *Success with the Gentle Art of Verbal Self-Defense,* (Englewood Cliffs, NJ: Prentice Hall, 1989), 4.

During my commutes to the university, I prayed that my fellow road warriors were too busy talking on their cell phones to observe my daffy expressions as I dutifully repeated each exercise demanded by my tape-recorded teacher. I began by buzzing my nose with a nasal "eeeeee" for as long as I could sustain the breath. Then, fish-faced with brows raised to hairline, I intoned soft "oh's" on various pitches as if my mind had just been miraculously filled with all the knowledge and wisdom of Athena. I "hmmmmmm"-ed to find a comfortable tone that tickled my lips, "hmmmmmmmmMa ma ma ma"-ed several times more, then whined in monotone witty phrases like, "MMMy mmmerry mmmom mmmade mmmarmalade," and "NNNo one knnnew nnnine nnnames."

Problems with the vocal mechanism are common among teachers, singers, and others who use their voices a great deal during the day. But it also turns out that more serious forms of vocal cord dysfunction have throughout history been associated with mental illness such as depression and personality disorders and even childhood sexual abuse. The term, *hysterical laryngitis*, reveals yet another fact about problems with the voice: vocal cord dysfunction occurs predominantly in young adult females.[*] In the nineteenth century, attacks of hysteria might include periods of vocal difficulty as well as wheezing and coughing, for which one contemporaneous medical text prescribed throwing cold water in the sufferer's face or holding smelling salts under the sufferer's nose. Longer term care for hysteria involved a reduced diet, exercise in fresh air, bathing in lukewarm water, "total avoidance of all sudden and violent emotions," and blood-letting.[†] While most of the treatment seems almost pleasant, I rather think the sight of a jar of leeches, writhing and ready to be pressed to my flesh, would be sufficient to bring on a bout of hysteria, a cause quite unrelated

---

[*]   Praveen Buddiga, MD, "Vocal Cord Dysfunction," eMedicine from WebMD, http://www.emediciine.com/med/topic3563.htm.

[†]   Robley Dunglison, M.D. *The Practice of Medicine or, A Treatise on Special Pathology and Therapeutics*. Volume 2. (Philadelphia: Lea & Blanchard, 1842), 326.

to my possession of a uterus or *hystera* in Latin, the root for both *hysteria* and *hysterectomy*, the surgical removal of a woman's womb.

"Company may, at it's [*sic*] election, … terminate Artist's employment in the event there is any material impairment of Artist's voice or any material change in Artist's present appearance," my contract in Las Vegas read. By those conditions, had I chosen to stay in Vegas I would long ago have lost my job as time began to touch my body. Had it been possible for me, childbearing would have been out of the question. Though few women are required by contract to submit to such control over their bodies, all professional women suffer similarly. Common wisdom speaks of the choice one has to make between family and career, and I imagine many have put off starting families until reaching some personally defined pinnacle in their careers.

Five years is a long time to audition, and acute awareness that you are daily failing to reach a bar that is ever being held higher can wreak havoc with your schedule and with your health. During my first year at the university, I took no days off—not even during the extended holidays between semesters. "Artist acknowledges that the services to be performed by Artist hereunder are of a special, unique, unusual and extraordinary character which gives them a peculiar value," my Vegas contract specified. I needed to prove the same thing was true to the academy, and while doing so I would have relished the clearly defined right to "a minimum of nine (9) hours off between the conclusion of work on one day and the commencement of work on the following day" that my dancer/singer's contract specified.

Life paints our bodies with experience. There are the noticeable scars: a line on my forehead marking how the skin split open and had to be stitched together when a childhood argument with my brother ended with my face smacking into the wall. There is another on my chin where a small tumor was surgically removed in my teens after years of misdiagnosis and treatment as a wart and after several unsuccessful de-witching attempts to remove it myself with a razor. A white hairline across the tip of my left index finger marks a grade school flirtation with suicide after my sister died. These are marks of survival, but it is the hidden scars—from loss, despair, and the unkindnesses of others—that threaten to disfigure the soul. It was time to lay down the burden of being, to embrace my past and imagine a new and brighter future. I would choose neither to change my decisions nor relive my youth for as I have cooled, I find the fire at my feet has given me purpose, tempered me, and made me strong.

14

OVA ~ HUEVOS ~ EGGS

Something bright and shiny flashed from beneath the truck bed as the pickup in front of me slowed. When the distance between our vehicles closed, I could see that the owner had enhanced his truck with the latest accessory: two large orbs slung in a silvery bag from the undercarriage, *chrome-plated bull balls.*

I really can't say that I comprehend what it is that compels a man to hang a large pair of testicles from the undercarriage of his pickup. Or, for that matter, to surgically implant silicone nuts in his dog when neutered, though according to the manufacturer, over 100,000 pets worldwide have received testicular implants, with no rejections.* The procedure reportedly preserves Fido's self esteem after emasculation, and no wonder, since a simple nut massage each week is recommended to prevent the buildup of scar tissue. A man must prove that he has *huevos;* a woman, when she bleeds, knows they have been given to her by God.

Angered by the blatant disparity in treatment I'd received at the university, I could remain silent no longer. To gain the same teaching privileges accorded other junior faculty members in our department required waging a small but vicious war. But at last—and with the support of a new department head—I was granted the opportunity to teach a course based on my research. The class was well-received by students, and my popularity rat-

---

*   CTI Corporation, "Neuticles: Testicular Implants for Dogs," http://www.neuti-cles.com.

ings, as measured by student evaluations, rose considerably. Yet I was left with no doubt that the moment of my victory was also my moment of defeat, as I observed in a bcc'd email that, according to an administrator, my course would be offered one time only: I should not expect the chance to teach it again. I resolved to leave the university (for what, I did not know). Nevertheless, at the urging of the department head, I decided to stay one more year and see the tenure game through.

What I wasn't prepared for was having to confront, at the same time, the possibility of a life-threatening ailment. If I had been asked before then where in my body I should worry most about the possibility of cancer, I would have named my female parts because of the years I'd spent avoiding gynecological exams despite recurrent breast discharge, several questionable pap tests, and persistent, undiagnosable abdominal pain. But it was my largest organ—my skin—that now gave me cause for concern.

Three scabs marked a mystery that began to plague me shortly after I submitted for final review my dossier and teaching portfolio, a veritable encyclopedia of my politically correct pedagogical life at the university. The perfectly round scabs dotted my skin, each slightly less than one-quarter inch in diameter. The one just below my right knee was a week older than the other two, and thus had had more time to heal. Yet because it was cut deepest, it was the most tender of the three. Its companion on my lower limb, a crusty red circle just above the ankle, hurt most when the small sample of flesh was taken, the anesthesia apparently no match for the rich supply of nerve endings that seemed to inhabit the area. The scab on my left forearm was surrounded by a sea of red, itchy blemishes.

My dermatologist, a wise and careful septuagenarian, was not able to explain why the skin on my feet and legs, my hands, my arms, my neck, and my back, erupted in so many angry welts, which after they'd made their presence known faded away if left alone, only to be replaced by others. He took a biopsy on my first visit, and observed that he thought the spots might be caused by some malfunction of my lymph system.

"There might be bad news," he gently remarked after collecting the first skin sample, but he was circumspect in revealing details and chose his words carefully as he wished to provoke in me neither alarm nor Google diagnosis. When I asked him to repeat the words he'd used when dictating his notes to the nurse, he spoke softly in a rich baritone that enveloped me like so many warm and comforting blankets, "Honey, I don't want you to go looking this up on the Internet. Let's wait for the test results."

In the meantime, the doctor asked me to eliminate the medication I took to strengthen my bones, the soy protein shakes I drank at breakfast, and the green tea I'd introduced to replace soft drinks. When the problem persisted, I began to keep inventory:

- January 11—New spots on right thumb, right forearm. About twenty on back of neck. Also left thumb, two places on forearm.

- January 16—New spots. Left foot (arch, little toe, heel). Left ankle, calf, left upper thigh.

He injected some chemical into a particularly bothersome eruption, stating that even though the pathologist's report had yet to arrive, he would have some idea about an appropriate diagnosis based on how my skin responded to the medication. The treated spot disappeared almost completely within hours but was soon followed by others.

- February 7—New spots on right thumb. General inventory: spots at back of neck, shoulders, arms, chest (some have faded); left calf, foot, toes; right ankle, foot, toes.

The next week there was very good news: tests were negative for lymphoma and leukemia. The pathologist's report suggested other possible causes: a virus, which my physician discounted because the problem had been going on too long; allergy to medication, which had been addressed when I gave up the bone medicine I'd been taking; and insect bites, which seemed unlikely as I could not recall being bitten. The other possibility that the doctor now mentioned was stress, whereupon I remarked that life had been somewhat challenging of late, though I was cautiously optimistic that circumstances would improve.

I neither offered nor did he ask for the details. But the facts were these: my application for tenure and promotion had received the unanimous endorsement of the department, and I'd just learned it had also been approved by the university-wide committee. With each round of approvals and the congratulations of those colleagues-in-the-know about this curiously public-yet-confidential process, I had begun to shed the years of tension and consider whether it might, indeed, be possible for me to make a career at the university. My overwhelming reaction was relief: I'd been grateful to believe the process was almost over as my energies were newly absorbed in other matters. Over Christmas, my mother's bipolar disorder had worsened suddenly and Dad (and all of us) worried that she would have to be committed. My nephew—who had yet to graduate from high school—required open-heart surgery that spring to correct a just-diagnosed birth defect. A corporate merger threatened my husband's position. With all of this, it was good to imagine I might have some job security for the coming year.

Nevertheless, the last line of the letter from the Provost, Chair of the University-wide Committee, gave me pause. He closed the missive with two simple statements: that "all positive recommendations have been forwarded to me for my review and recommendation" and that "Further action will be reported as it occurs."

Two weeks later, I received a call from the department secretary. "Kevin wants to know if you can come up for a meeting with the Dean at one o'clock," she said in a chipper, professionally impenetrable tone. In all my years at the university, this was a first, notable not only for the short notice, given my commute to campus from a city nearby, but also for the announced presence of the Dean at the impromptu meeting. It was sort of like being told that judgment day had arrived and St. Peter and Jesus himself would be meeting me at the pearly gates.

"Of course," I replied pleasantly, "Do we know what this is about?"

"Kevin said you'd know," she responded.

I entered the department office and saw that the Dean and the department head were already seated in the inner sanctum. "Come sit down," Kevin said, not hesitating long enough for his secretary to show me in. He closed the office door behind me.

He handed me a white envelope stamped in red, CONFIDENTIAL, and before I could open it, he and the Dean launched simultaneously into words of regret and reassurance. I tried to listen to them and respond politely and at the same time, to carefully read what the Provost had written.

"Regrettably," the Provost stated, "your dossier does not contain sufficient objective evidence" that I had performed my duties to his standards and should be granted tenure. He was contemplating overruling the dozens of people across campus who had reviewed my work and advanced my application.

The Provost hadn't yet made up his mind, though, and if I liked, I could submit any additional material beyond the dossier that the previous two committees might have considered during their evaluations. Otherwise, he would simply make up his mind based on what was in the twenty-page dossier, the confidential review letters from respected scholars in my discipline, and the lengthy recommendation letter Kevin had written months ago.

"It's all in there," I heard Kevin continue as my attention shifted away from the page and back to the people seated before me. He shook his head. "The evidence is in my letter and in your dossier. I really don't know what's going on here."

I sat there, stone-faced, and flatly remarked, "I guess I have a decision to make." There was a limit to how much more of this institutional hazing I would put up with. Submit nothing else and the game was over: the Provost's letter would be my pink slip. You see, an unsuccessful tenure bid is merely an abstract way of informing you of a very concrete reality: after five years of slavish effort, you have been fired, your career is over, and the likelihood of being hired at another university is slim. It's time again for a career change, so *buck up,* baby, and don't let the door bang you on the butt when you leave.

Kevin blustered with surprise at my response, "Well, I hope you *do* submit your teaching portfolio," he said, "Otherwise I'll be up the proverbial creek." Was he thinking of how hard it would be to find a replacement to teach my courses, given how short-staffed our program already was? "You've got an excellent portfolio, and it's important for you to see this through to set a standard for others."

I spent little more than one angry hour that night composing the cover letter that would accompany the four-inch binder of evidence I'd compiled over five long years on the tenure track to document my teaching skills. I thanked the Provost for the opportunity to submit the work then listed and summarized the binder's contents in six pages of excruciating detail that any lawyer would love.

- February 14—Inventory: spots on right foot, ankle, calf. Left foot, ankle, calf. Left forearm. Right hand and forearm. Back. Neck.

- February 15—New spot: large, itchy welt (one and one-half inches in diameter) on right arm.

A shot of cortisone calmed my symptoms down, but the bothersome red spots had returned twenty-four hours after I concluded a one-week treatment regimen. "I hate to attribute this to stress," the doctor noted, still unwilling to abdicate diagnosis to a catchall cause. Neither the antihistamine he'd prescribed nor the dietary changes had any effect. It was time for another biopsy, to ensure that the first-round results were correct.

- February 21—Large welt on right pinkie finger, 1-inch long. Large welt on left forearm, one-half inch in diameter.

The skin sample had been damaged at the lab and was unusable; the doctor took two new samples and sent them for analysis.

Two days later, I spied a tiny insect skittering across my pillow as I made the bed. I dashed into the kitchen, where I hastily retrieved a small plastic container for trapping the intruder.

A quick search and a few taps on my touchpad later, and I had solved the mystery. My conclusions were soon confirmed by the exterminator who arrived that afternoon:

- February 23—Bedbugs—Captured!

"I have my diagnosis," I crowed when I next saw the doctor and showed him my trophy, still trapped in its small plastic cage. My husband was certainly being bitten too, but it seems I am slightly allergic (and a lot less hairy) thus the bites showed up more dramatically on my skin. I was so relieved to know at last that I did not have some strange and fatal disease that I was oblivious to the embarrassment I might have felt about having vermin in my home. The doctor referred to the insects obliquely as he dictated notes for my case, and discharged me from care unless the spots remained after the insects were gone.

The exterminator couldn't tell us exactly when or how our home could have become infested. There were numerous possibilities: there were several infested apartments in a building across the street and the public schools were apparently having terrible problems. An insect might have hitched a ride when one of us had traveled recently, as bedbugs sometimes make cozy homes in hotel rooms. Another possible source was second-hand furniture, but we hadn't bought any in years. We finally concluded that the pests most likely arrived as stowaways in the truck that delivered our new mattress after having picked up an old, contaminated mattress somewhere earlier along the route.

It took four days to prepare our small apartment for treatment. I thought that if we were meticulous from the beginning we might shorten what I understood could be a protracted process to eliminate the pests (there were two treatments scheduled, one month apart). We began in the bedroom by discarding everything that had been on the floor beneath the bed, telephone and all, because the flat, tiny insects will breed in the slightest crevice that offers shelter, including home electronics. We stripped the bed and washed every stitch of bedclothes—sheets, blankets, pillow covers, shams—then put the cleaned items in oversized zipper-sealed plastic bags. We removed the mattress and foundation from the bed frame and, since our brand new, expensive foam mattress could be damaged by the insecticides the exterminator would use, we sealed it inside a huge plastic moving bag and leaned both mattress and foundation against one wall. Then we inspected the bed frame, where we found evidence of the insects: tiny black spots near the joints on the frame where they defecated immediately after feeding on our blood at night while we slept. I shuddered as I thought of all the flickery little itches that had sometimes kept me from falling quickly to sleep and realized they were doubtless caused by the insects arriving for a succulent meal. We vacuumed the frame and the dressers, then pulled the furniture away from the walls.

Up to this point, I'd been able to avoid completely freaking out because I had been assured that our infestation was fairly minor, as the exterminator hadn't found any live insects when he inspected. I'm the kind of person who can neither bear insects nor killing them because I'm utterly horrified by the crunch-squishing sound and feel of the rupturing exoskeleton at death. But the calm and industrious zeal with which I'd approached the necessary cleaning soon evaporated. Where the floor met the wall behind the headboard, the carpeting was alive with insects, an ocean of them, crawling their way up and down the carpet fibers in hideous waves. I shuddered and briefly closed my eyes, then gritted my teeth and aimed my weapon, grateful that my vacuum cleaner was the old-fashioned kind with an interior bag that could be discarded so I wouldn't have to witness their whirling dance inside the machine and then deal with scooping them from the chamber for disposal in a sealed plastic bag to prevent spreading the infestation.

After vacuuming and hurriedly sealing and discarding the vacuum cleaner bag to make sure none of the insects escaped, we pulled down the draperies and bagged them for freezing. Anything that couldn't be laundered had to be dry-cleaned or frozen, so our woolens and down comforter spent two weeks in the deep freeze next to the ice cream and frozen hamburger to kill any bugs that might be dwelling therein. We emptied the dresser drawers and closets, piling any items we didn't anticipate needing right away into laundry hampers and began to wash, fold, and seal the clean clothing in plastic bags, a process that would continue for weeks. We stacked the bags of clean clothing in laundry baskets and plastic storage boxes since the dressers and closets needed to be empty for treatment. We were merciless in discarding clutter as we attacked the rest of the apartment, and piles of books, newspapers, and magazines that might offer the insects shelter headed for the landfill. We bagged throw pillows and afghans for freezing. We vacuumed the floors and the walls and the furniture. And we spent three blissful, bug-free nights on the airbed in the living room, naively believing the worst was over.

The morning after the exterminator's first treatment, we awoke refreshed from restful slumber only to discover that the insects had made the journey from the bedroom to the living room. Once again, we'd become the local bedbug buffet. There were new spots on my skin and small bloodstains on the sheets, which I now knew to look for. We stripped the bed and began (again) to wash all of the bedclothes. We vacuumed the carpet, the living room furniture, and the air mattress, then showered and dressed for work. "It's normal to see insects after a treatment," the exterminator told me when I finally had the chance to call. "The EPA controls the chemicals we use, and they aren't nearly as strong as the DDT they used in the 1950s."

Thus began our all-out war with the invaders. I became hunter as well as the hunted, studying the bedclothes each morning as a trapper studies the ground for scat, and as I moved through the apartment for my morning routine scanning the floors, walls, and ceilings like an eagle searches the ground for prey. As we waited the thirty days before the next scheduled treatment, I began to keep a new inventory:

- March 3—Live insect near ceiling in bedroom

- March 4—Live insect on bed, spots on sheets, bites on hands, legs. Dead bedbug next to dining table in living room. Two live bugs on ceiling in bedroom. One (live) near window. One (dead) in bathroom.

- March 5—One (live) on robe (in bathroom). One on bed. One in bathroom near light switch.

It turns out that the pesticides irritate the insects (!) and tend to flush them from their hiding places, thus the appearance that the infestation was growing worse, not better. Each new sighting—of evidence or insect—stimulated another round of vacuuming and laundry (several loads of bedclothes alone almost daily).

It could take days for the poisoned insects to sicken and die—during which they might enjoy several nightly snacks on our bodies—so I began frustrated experiments with new weapons to smash the bugs when I found them. I tried to use a broom handle to eliminate bugs I saw on the walls and the ceiling, but they were too fast for my awkward jabs and the rounded end of the stick couldn't reach into the tight corners where they inevitably sought safety. I chased around after one too-lively bug on the carpet with a pair of needle-nose pliers, finally trying to crush the beast with my shoe, only to discover that he had crawled into the crevices of the molded sole, from which I extricated and eliminated him with the needle noses.

Finally, I discovered the most potent weapon for hand-to-bug combat: duct tape. Even an insect scurrying across a textured ceiling is no match for this weapon as with the slightest contact any tiny invader becomes permanently affixed to the sticky tape. No need to squish them either: just fold the two sides together with the bugs wrapped securely inside and throw the tidy package away. It's also ideal for dealing with the eggs. It wasn't until we completely disassembled the bed frame in preparation for the second scheduled visit from the exterminator that we finally located the nursery: tiny clusters of white dots glued to the wood beneath the joining brackets. We removed the bedbug eggs from the wooden crossbars by placing a length of duct tape over the clusters, rubbing the tape lightly to ensure good contact, and ripping off the tape and eggs.

Even if I had felt I had trusted friends at the university, I don't think I would have mentioned the bedbugs, in part because of the stigma an infestation carries, and in part because the Provost's inaction on my tenure case magnified my sense of social isolation on campus. Though technically a confidential matter, there were dozens of people who knew before I did that the Provost had found me to be less than acceptable, because the letter notifying me was, by policy, sent also to the members of the university-wide committee.

My circumstances were made semi-public in early February when the names and photos of all of the newly tenured and promoted faculty members were published in the campus paper, at which point my time in the pillory began. Everyone who knew I had gone up for tenure could see that I hadn't made the cut. I believed my sentence would last one month, based on the deadline the Provost had specified in his letter (he indicated that he would "defer any decision until March 2"). But March 2 had come and gone with nary a word from on high and no key to release me. I began to wonder if during the time I'd spent waiting in the stocks my body had vanished away completely (and in some ways it had, as I had taken to keeping my office door shut unless I was meeting with students. I was also spending as little time on campus as possible just to have time enough to combat the pests at home. I knew I could neither field questions nor questioning glances without dissolving into tears). Whatever sentiments others might have had about the matter, they were gagged by the pretense of confidentiality. They weren't supposed to know and thus weren't allowed to speak. It took every ounce of physical and emotional reserve in my bones to meet my responsibilities to the university honorably and with the composure of the wrongly condemned.

It's an odd day when an economist tells an English teacher how to interpret the language. But that's exactly what happened when, after seven weeks of silent "deliberation" by the Provost and my careful scrutiny of the policies and procedures manual, I finally inquired about pursuing the only recourse that seemed available to me: filing a grievance to request action. My years of training and experience in analyzing, crafting, and teaching others to use the language were dismissed summarily as the faculty facilitator repeated the party line, seemingly coached by university counsel and following the example set so often by our country's leaders: when you make a promise you later fail to keep, find another way to interpret the language and claim to have been misunderstood. The Provost, I was to learn, meant by "defer[ing] his decision" that March 2 was the deadline for me to submit additional materials. He would decide whenever he decided, and he would take all the time he wished.

The good thing about a bedbug infestation is that it pretty much takes your mind off everything else that's going on in life. The longer it persists, the steelier must be your resolve. There's no other way, because you can't just move away from the problem unless you leave behind all you are and all you own. Take any of your possessions with you and you risk bringing the insects along for the ride as well.

The Provost's next communication was limply congratulatory, a sterile notice that he'd recommended me for tenure and a flaccid welcome to the rank of associate professor, one of only two promotions a faculty member might anticipate in a lifelong academic career. It was a bitter release from the years of hard time I'd put in, and a "success" that could not wash clean the past nor vanquish the thoughts of revenge I'd sometimes harbored as he toyed so carelessly with my career. To ease such tensions, I recommend the game, "Boss Toss" for those who are similarly frustrated at work. The special gun comes with painted plastic boss-shaped "bullets"—one-and-one-half-inch men and women in business attire—that can be launched headlong from the firing mechanism toward the included target, which you may have attached to the back of your office door or the side of your cubicle where, after impact, the bosses can bounce, quite satisfactorily and repeatedly, into the garbage. Nevertheless, I was disturbed to think that I now knew why, when action seems futile and communication is cut off, people seek to solve workplace problems with violence.

Rumor had it that long before he'd even seen the stack of applications for tenure and promotion, the Provost had arbitrarily decided to pull some aside to demonstrate that he could make the tough decisions. I learned through the grapevine that there were at least four of us, mostly women, whose lives he'd kept on hold. Ultimately, eight full months had passed since I'd first submitted my paperwork for review, eight weeks of which were spent waiting to learn whether the Provost would welcome me for eternity or banish me forever, and another three before the decision was official, endorsed by a vote of the Board of Trustees. All of us were promoted in the end, an outcome that only emphasized the needlessness of the Provost's delay. I thought of sending him a nice gift to acknowledge my gratitude for his special attention, but I thought he might not understand what to do with a pair of shiny, stainless steel emasculators, the specially designed surgical instruments used to castrate bulls.

15

LISTENING WHEN THE BODY SPEAKS

The same day I received the Provost's congratulatory letter I awoke to find two new insect bites on my chest near my heart. Knowing when you've seen your last bedbug is like knowing when you've had your last period: a long time must pass without evidence and you still might not be quite sure it's all over.

In my years at the university, I had aged visibly and developed myriad physical ailments, including heart palpitations and chest pain severe enough to constrict my breathing and cause dizzy spells that some days required me use the wall for support as I made my way down the hall. I felt unremitting fatigue and often had to lie down on the floor of my office to rest during the day. I had difficulty sleeping, and sometimes woke in the night as my body temperature shifted from ice to fire and back again. "I thought I was going through early menopause," remarked a colleague who was unaware of my physical discomforts during a conversation one day about the university and the tenure process. The same was certainly true for me.

It turns out that there is a cyst on my left ovary suspicious enough to bump up the date for my new patient appointment with one of best women gynecologists in the city from October to July, just two weeks away. I'm not too worried, though. I walked this road twenty years ago, after Vegas and before the university, and I know what to expect and what to ask for. If there must be another laparoscopy, I'll insist they wait at least until I am conscious before they require me to sign the discharge papers. I won't permit them to wheel me to the curb and just dump me in the back seat of the car for the long trip home, and I'll demand to have some adequate means for killing the crippling pain I felt in my back and shoulders when I finally regained consciousness in my bed.

In the weeks that passed before my recommendation for tenure was publicly announced in the campus paper, I noticed a change among some of my colleagues, most of whom, after six long years, were still strangers to me. The previous year—after I'd requested my right to respond to an "error in fact or omission" in my annual review—the department head revealed to me that my colleagues thought me aloof. I told him the truth: I had simply quit speaking after experience had taught me caution and my efforts to strike up conversation had been shunned. He must have said a few quiet words within the department because once, when my office door was open a little longer than usual, one of the other writing instructors stopped by to chat. He asked how I used the flip chart paper on the easel that dominated the far wall of my office. "I use it to take notes when my students talk about their writing," I replied. "I put their words up here while they speak so we can see their ideas …" I finished the statement in my thoughts, "and together we can find their truths." Several others went out of their way to include me in an end-of-term celebration, and asked permission during the party to toast to my success.

Although I have been accepted as a lifetime member of this strange and psychotic club, I cannot yet imagine committing myself to staying beyond the next year and must trust the future will sort itself out. Despite years of study and scholarship—and even some national recognition for my work along the way—I have suspected all along I am at heart a fraud. The things I feel I know best are things that I have lived, the things I know in my flesh: I can still dance the time step I learned almost thirty years ago to begin "Tea for Two." I can tango with only a slight refresher and some coaxing of forgotten muscles. I can recognize eating disorders in some of my students. I understand pain and fear.

Modern technology has displaced the old marquee that once identified the hotel and advertised the show, still playing twenty-five years after it finally opened eight months after the fire. The block letter sign has been replaced by an interactive marquee with three giant programmable screens, one on top of another stacked like so many children's blocks. Selected video clips featuring the bodies of beautiful, nearly nude women bedecked in hundreds of thousands of rhinestones flash across the bottom-most screen to lure customers to the show. The top two screens are devoted to a posterior view of one of the dancers, clothed only in a jeweled g-string and fishnet tights, her shoulders and arms draped with a feather boa and a chain dripping with glittering Swarovski crystals. Though still displayed on the sign, the producer's name has been eclipsed by the main attraction just as the hotel itself, once the largest in the world, has been eclipsed by even grander mega-resorts up the road.

A lot has changed in twenty-five years. Although creamy flesh still dominates, the cast has been integrated, the "colored" dancers no longer segregated in separate, stereotyped numbers ("I think I'll scream if I get another bow on my butt," a black dancer once muttered after a costume fitting). The cast was smaller, too, and the show itself had been downsized, the extravaganza now significantly less extravagant, a relic of another era, its splendor diminished in comparison to newer entertainments. It has even gone "dark" on Friday evenings, displaced by more wholesome fare, a Vegas version of a television game show.

For the first time since the fire, I stepped upon the stage, walked to the wings, and descended the steps toward the dressing rooms. "The performers do fifty to sixty flights of stairs for each show," our host for the backstage tour explained. He was one of the chorus dancers, tall and slender, handsome in a tuxedo with sequined jacket.

"Most of the costumes are original," he said as he showed us one of the jeweled evening gowns used in the show. It wasn't one that I remembered.

"Weren't the costumes damaged during the fire?" I asked.

He dismissed my question. "The fire happened the year before the show began its run," he said, explaining briefly that once there had been a big fire at the hotel for those who would not have remembered.

"I'm sorry, but I must differ" I insisted, "The show was in rehearsal at the time of the fire. I know because I was there. I was in the show." I blushed as I spoke, conscious of my dowdy appearance, hair frizzled and sweaty from our walk along the strip that summer morning, tourist clothes rumpled from the time they'd spent in the suitcase.

"Oh yeah," he said, "I think I heard that they had dress rehearsal the night before the fire." And he quickly changed the subject, shifting to facts about how many people work to keep the wardrobe in repair, even mending rips in the fishnet tights with thread scavenged from worn-out pairs to avoid the appearance of scars and to keep the costume color consistent from one cast member to another. Body tattoos and piercings, now common, had to be covered with special makeup. As the tour continued, I began to notice the wear on the costumes, still spectacular but showing their age. Some of the feathers were slightly bent and bedraggled, a few rhinestones were missing here and there, and the black satin cover on a jacket button was worn through to the metal base.

"The men aren't completely left out when it comes to the fancy costumes," he said as he showed us a sparkling vest, a copy of which he'd be wearing that night in the show. "I don't know how the story got started, but there's supposedly six hundred and sixty-six rhinestones on each one." He continued his congenial patter, "Some of the dancers would pry off a rhinestone or two because 666 is thought to be an unlucky number."

As our host spoke of life in the show—auditions every six months to keep your job, rehearsals from midnight to four in the morning—I began to see with different eyes what I had missed by leaving Las Vegas, and for once I was glad to have left the glitter and the grind behind.

There's a grand old lady across the street from the bus stop in an aging urban neighborhood near where I live. She has marble columns, stained-glass windows, a wide and inviting porch, and finely chiseled features. The ruddy paint used to brighten her aging brick face has been carelessly applied, lending an artificial blush to the limestone and washing off in areas affected by too much moisture. Air conditioners rudely interrupt tall, second-story windows, and judging from the cracked wooden frames and the aluminum foil covering the panes of glass, third floor rooms are neglected and unused.

As I waited for the bus in front of the hospital, I admired this grand old home. This lady, too, was somewhat in need of attention, but, I thought, *still* she is grand, and she is grand *because* she is old and has survived. She is part of my city's charm, lending warmth and an enduring presence. Her ample proportions and generous curves speak of welcoming neighbors and having room in her heart for all those who would enter. As much as anything else, it was the lady and her neighbors who beckoned us to join them in the heart of the city.

My childhood included contact with several generations of elder women whom I have treasured—grandmothers, a great-grandmother, plus several aunts and great-aunts. Time marked them as different from me and different from one another; indeed I think I would have found it confusing if through contemporary artifice and technology they had looked to be of a single, youthful generation, like a suburban neighborhood populated by antiseptic, Stepford architecture.

As I have begun to feel my own body touched by time, I have struggled to find a balance between the imposed cultural standard of perpetual youth and my fond memories of generational difference among my female progenitors. But witnessing these changes come to be wrought upon my own body has challenged my sense of being as to my eyes I look more each day like a cartoon of myself with prominent features achieving unwilling exaggeration.

For some, the gradual loss of fertility denoted by the language we use to describe this later phase of a woman's life—menopause and perimeno-pause, *the change*, the climacteric—marks cyclical changes with loss of self. Yet when I look at photos of my female elders, their eyes are not empty but brimming with wit, with wisdom, and with the strength that comes from knowing this too shall pass.

The grand old lady across the street requires a little more care than a newly built home, but in return, she shelters knowing secrets in the wear in her floorboards and banisters. Living with her takes more effort, but offers rewards no younger soul can match.

As fecundity wanes in echoes of pubescent upheaval, we should not see the end of menstruation as marking a reversal in vitality but rather we should honor this period as *probity*, a time in which the changes in our bodies challenge us to live by our highest ideals. I have been fortunate that there have been many strong women in my family, some of whom have lived long enough for me to know them as nonagenarians and centenari-ans. If my ancestors offer any advice, perhaps it is that autumn is the most colorful season of a woman's existence.

Once, when marveling at my sister's vocal prowess, my father quietly mused, "I always thought you would be the singer, Katherine." My mother echoed his sentiment at the end of a particularly difficult phone conversation when, after my father got off the line, I lamented that he seemed unable to recall any joyful moments from my childhood. "I remember lots of things," my mother said, "I remember that you have an absolutely beautiful voice."

AFTERWORD

For any event, many truths can be spoken: guidance may be experienced as constraint, or victory felt as defeat. But that which is written and shared and *kept* takes on special significance. The letter we found in the old family trunk was one such example. "Dear Mother," it began,

> Your letter so full of a mother's tender sympathy reached us this morning. These words assured us of the love and sympathy of a mother's heart and brought forth tears of gratitude for such words and such a mother. It was just three weeks ago today when our little Mabel was taken sick. Charlie was gone, having started for Deadwood the night before to attend Supreme Court.

Aunt Olive's crabbed scrawl on the outside of the envelope identified the letter as being from "Aunt Edna, Uncle Charlie's wife, to his mother, Grandma Templeton, after the death of their oldest daughter of diphtheria in 1889." The story Edna told of Mabel's death became the family narrative, the Truth about those tragic fall days during which Mabel first fell sick and quickly became morbidly ill while her father was out of town. A telegram reached Charlie too late for him to catch the next train, delaying his return to Edna's side for several agonizing days.

> Mabel grew worse and Wednesday night about twelve o'clock I sent for the doctor, and when he came in he thought she was dying. Another physician was called in. We bolstered her up with pillows, watched and tended her all through the night and towards morning she began to rally. She seemed so much better on Friday and I felt so hopeful. Charlie reached home at nine o'clock that evening and Oh! how glad we were to see him, and how glad he was to be home. Mabel knew him and talked to him and he brought her a new doll but she was too weak to hold it.

It was about three o'clock on Saturday when she began to fail. We sent for another physician but no human power could help her. The doctor stayed all night and about half past two o'clock Sunday morning she breathed her last.

Mom met Dad at the car when he and a friend in the driver's seat pulled up in front of the house after a grief-stricken drive home from the northern part of the state where Dad was working that summer. My parents embraced, and then spoke in hushed tones as they walked from the curb to the front door while I trailed behind them. Certain arrangements had to be discussed.

"Do you want to see her?" my mother asked.

How sweet and happy she looked with the little white dress which she used to wear to Sunday school. Her little white casket was laden with flowers and while only two dear friends beside the minister ventured inside the house to mingle their tears with ours, a long line of carriages was waiting outside to accompany us to the cemetery. Sunday was a beautiful autumn day and heaven seemed to smile its benediction upon all of us.

"No," my father replied, "I want to remember her the way she was when she was alive." Amy's casket would be closed, but I think the beautiful pink granite gravestone Mom and Dad selected for Amy helped to ease their grief. Ornamented with a sleeping lamb, the stone proclaims that Amy was "A Happy Child."

"God only knows how hard it was for us to part with our darling, and how lonely our home is without her," Aunt Edna wrote.

In the midst of our sorrow there is sweet comfort in the thought that her suffering is ended and she hath passed through the pearly gates to a brighter home above. We know she loves us still and stands waiting to welcome us. We feel sure that her little life was spared to us a few days longer that her papa might reach her bedside. How thankful we are for that, and for the sweet life which she was given.

After she was buried, we never spoke of Amy's death. The family narrative has inevitably been, therefore, fragmentary, individual, and colored by our own emotions, experiences, and perceptions. How different would our lives have been if we could have composed together the story of Amy's death, filled with grief, with love, with forgiveness, and even with gratitude as Aunt Edna had done?

I write for myself a new narrative, one that tells the truths that until now I did not know. Let me tell you of Lizzie, who learned to talk only after Amy was no longer there to see to her needs, the only one of us to speak her grief aloud. "Where's Amy? Where's Amy?" she asked in her toddler's voice for weeks after Amy died. Let me tell you of my brother, my brave big brother who found my sister and tried to save her life by pulling her to safety, away from the wires, the water, the currents. Let me tell you of my mother, the clear-minded, decisive woman who knelt in the grass and pressed trembling lips to Amy's small mouth, trying to breathe life into her lifeless body after she directed us to call for help. Let me tell you of my father, who couldn't bear the loss of any one of his children and who mourns my sister still.

"We are all well," the last paragraph began.

Had our storm sash put on today and our coal bin filled so you see we are preparing for winter. Please write us often and tell Lill and Abby that we thank them for their words of sympathy and love. Charlie joins me in sending love to you all. Your loving daughter, Edna.

978-0-595-48416-4
0-595-48416-6

Printed in the United States
113277LV00005B/232-291/P

9 780595 484164